THE BEST IN MEDICINE

THE BEST
IN MEDICINE

$$\bullet \blacksquare \bullet$$

How and Where to Find the Best
Health Care Available

HERBERT J. DIETRICH, M.D.
AND VIRGINIA H. BIDDLE

HARMONY BOOKS / NEW YORK

Published by Harmony Books, a division of Crown Publishers, Inc., 201 East 50th Street, New York, New York 10022. Member of the Crown Publishing Group.

HARMONY and colophon are trademarks of Crown Publishers, Inc.

Manufactured in the United States of America

Library of Congress Cataloging-in-Publication Data

Dietrich, Herbert J.
   The best in medicine: how and where to find the best health care available /
Herbert J. Dietrich and Virginia H. Biddle.—Rev. and updated ed.
      p.   cm.
   1. Hospitals—United States—Directories.   2. Medicine—Specialties and specialists—United States—Directories. 3. Medical care—United States—Directories.
4. Medicine—Information services—United States——Directories. I. Biddle, Virginia H.   II. Title.
   [DNLM: 1. Health Facilities—United States—directories.   2. Health Facilities—United States—popular works.   3. Hospitals, Special—United States—directories.
4. Hospitals, Special—United States—popular works.   WX 22 AA1 D56b]
RA977.D43   1990
362.1'1'02573—dc20
DNLM/DLC
for Library of Congress   90-4232
                                                                              CIP

ISBN 0-517-57554-X

10 9 8 7 6 5 4 3 2 1

Revised Edition

CONTENTS

ACKNOWLEDGMENTS

The authors are deeply grateful to the many physicians—all eminent in their respective fields—who took the time to answer the questionnaire from which these lists were compiled. Almost as a rule, the more prominent and busier the doctor, the more thorough and detailed the response. We also wish to thank the numerous institutions, public and private, from which we obtained information regarding graduate training programs, hospital accreditation, rehabilitation facilities, and the current research into a variety of diseases.

Among the individuals who have provided us with strong support for this project are the following: Elizabeth Day, former librarian of Good Samaritan Hospital in West Palm Beach, Florida, and her successor, Linda O'Callaghan; Lawrence Whitacre of the Commission on Accreditation of Rehabilitation Facilities; Florence Antoine of the National Cancer Institute's communication office; and Alexander W. Biddle, whose unfailing encouragement and help with much of the research were indispensable to the completion of this work. Finally, we wish to express our appreciation to our editor, Margaret Garigan, for her patience and many helpful suggestions in preparing this updated, revised edition.

INTRODUCTION

The Best in Medicine directs patients in need of treatment for serious illness to the best doctors and hospital centers in America, as selected by top American doctors themselves. Specifically, these medical centers and their affiliated hospitals were named by over 300 American medical specialists, including hospital administrators, professors of medicine, and scientific researchers.

They were asked, "Where would *you* go if you or a member of your family were in need of the best available health care?" Their answers (excluding their own centers of practice) are listed throughout this book, along with a combined list of *the 25 best U.S. hospitals* and medical centers.

Until recently, so-called medical miracles were extremely rare, apparently resulting more from faith in the supernatural than from the magic of medicine. Today, however, they are frequent and occur every day in medical centers where the united goal is the best possible health care and where, by virtue of the sheer numbers of patients treated annually, health practitioners have perfected medical skills and sharpened perceptions. Whereas your local internist or surgeon sees perhaps 50 patients a year with similar cases of a specific illness, those on staffs of teaching hospitals see and treat hundreds.

These miracles are also made possible, of course, by steady advances in biology, genetics, and chemistry laboratories; by the invention of new instruments to aid in more precise diagnoses; and by the ever-increasing knowledge of doctors in all specialties. Ultimately, though, skilled specialists and surgeons, aided by trained teams of experts and the new instruments and equipment available in the best hospitals, accomplish medical miracles.

Your local family physician will gladly refer you to the right medical center for whatever further treatment is needed in a medical crisis. Or you can find where to go and learn more about your illness and the most expert and newest treatments among the lists in the following pages.

We arrived at our conclusions by sending questionnaires to ten representative doctors in each of the 25 medical specialty categories. Each was asked to list ten hospitals of outstanding excellence for his or her own specialty excluding his or her own base of operation and regardless of geographical location. The doctors were then asked to list three areas of specific expertise for each hospital chosen.

In addition, we personally interviewed a number of doctors who specialize in those fields about which more information was needed than the questionnaires could provide. We then consulted statistics pertaining to the postgraduate training programs of those medical institutions accredited by the Accreditation Council for Graduate Medical Education. Using the data from all these sources, we compiled a list of approximately 20 medical centers of excellence for each category.

Beyond inclusion in the main lists, we did not feel it possible to rank hospitals in order of excellence, except for the number of times individual hospitals appeared on the filled-out questionnaires. In any case, we hope you will bear in mind that institutions and individuals not appearing on these lists may well be comparable to—or may even surpass—those listed herein. Those medical centers listed were rated "excellent" in a broader number of areas. We believe that this book is truly a complete guide to the best medical care available in the United States.

THE BEST
IN MEDICINE

Nor bring to see me cease to live
Some doctor full of phrase and fame
To shake his sapient head and give
The ill he cannot cure, a name.

"A Wish"
Matthew Arnold

· 1 ·
THE CHOICE IS YOURS

Most people today are aware of the marvelous advances being made in medical science. In fact, many of us have been stirred by these reports to give some vague thought to our own and our family's possible future need for the best available medical treatments for a serious illness.

But if that need arises suddenly, as it most often does, we panic. We cannot find the clippings or the information we've saved, nor can we remember the names of doctors and hospitals we've heard of or read about. Instead, we do the easiest thing and call the local paramedics for a fast trip to the nearest hospital emergency room where the only medical specialist available at the moment takes over—all of which is as it should be in a crisis.

Without a personal physician upon whom you can absolutely rely, however, you—or your wife, husband, child, or parent—may often be rushed into emergency surgery and treatment with little time for (or thought of) expert consultation and a more complete knowledge on the part of the attending physician of the individual patient. The occasional tragic result of this course of action brings us to the first and most important medical rule: *Choose a personal physician—more specifically a general practitioner—with good credentials from a top-flight medical school and from hospitals with good internship and residency training programs.*

In some areas, particularly large urban centers and remote geographic areas of the country, general practitioners are in short supply. With the increasing prestige of general practice and its many inducements for young physicians to select it as a career, however, this situation is slowly beginning to turn around. Indeed, economic necessity will push this trend. In an era of declining population growth, oversupply is beginning to dim both the allure and the financial rewards for young, highly trained specialists just entering practice. Quite a few of these young doctors are turning to general practice as a means of earning their livelihood.

It is not a contradiction in terms to speak of the *specialty* of general practice.

1

These days it is usual, but not mandatory, for even a general practitioner to have one or more years of graduate training beyond medical school and internship. There is now a Board of Family Practice that certifies competence in general practice on the basis of graduate work, continuing education programs, and an examination that tests doctors on their knowledge of medicine as it relates to the family. (There are, however, many excellent general practitioners who do not choose formal recognition of their abilities by the certifying board.)

Many people choose to have an internist (a specialist in internal medicine) as their family physician. This, however, is not the best arrangement. The young internist, apart from his or her own specialty, does not have as broad a knowledge as the experienced generalist. Remember, an internist is a diagnostic specialist and not a more extensively trained general practitioner.

There are a number of other reasons why you should have a general practitioner as your primary-care doctor. First of all, in the vast majority of cases, the general practitioner *will* be able to diagnose and treat your condition. For the more difficult problems, however, he or she will usually know, on the basis of results with other patients, which specialists are best equipped to handle a given problem. In the past, the general practitioner was usually present at any specialty consultation, and the specialist would usually not consent to see a patient without the permission of the personal physician. These ethics, somewhat in disuse today, are not merely good manners but also are a means of protecting the patient. With such an arrangement, everyone concerned knows what is going on; without it, the patient could be in jeopardy.

Nowadays there is also a somewhat dangerous tendency for patients to assume the responsibility of selecting specialists for a given condition on their own. There may be little or no communication between the specialist and the primary-care physician, or, for that matter, among the several specialists the patient may be consulting at the same time. Too often the result is that the patient is given medicines by three or four doctors—medicines that may be incompatible with each other or dangerous when prescribed and taken at the same time. Medicines may be recommended by any number of specialists, but *one* doctor, the personal physician, should be the *only* prescriber or the monitor of all medications. Whether in the hospital or out, this rule should be strictly adhered to.

Another frequent disadvantage of sidestepping the general practitioner and consulting a specialist on your own is the overinvestigation of what may be a less serious complaint before any general examination of the patient. For example, if a patient suffering from a series of headaches first consults a neurologist or a neurosurgeon, a brain scan (costing $300 to $400) will almost inevitably be ordered to check for the possibility of a brain tumor. Tumors, however, are one of the rarer causes of headaches. It usually makes more sense for the patient, after a complete general examination, to be treated through such medical means as tranquilizers or muscle relaxants before proceeding, if necessary, to more extensive investigations of the cause. Sometimes, too, the patient wastes valuable time and money by visiting specialist after specialist and receiving a number of narrow views of his or her problem.

How does one go about choosing a personal physician? Usually, the recommendations of trusted friends will give you the names of highly regarded local doctors. All too often, however, the leading doctors in the community are difficult, and sometimes impossible, to see. Furthermore, with their heavy patient loads, they usually do not have the necessary time to devote to new patients.

Why not investigate a newer doctor in the community? Young doctors with good credentials whose practices are not yet too busy bring to their patients a number of assets: recent training, up-to-date knowledge of diagnostic and treatment methods, and the essential time to study their patients' problems. These assets may be preferable to the work of an experienced doctor who is rushed and overbooked and are highly preferable to treatment by a prominent doctor who has grown tired from overwork.

Never choose a doctor on the basis of hearsay alone or because he or she has a winning personality. Find out the facts about any doctor in your area with a simple call to the county medical society where he or she is in practice. When you ask for any doctor's background, the basic credentials will be furnished to you at once with no questions asked. You will then have done all the necessary checking on his or her medical training and experience. The rest is up to your own intuitive judgment.

Given a doctor with the best credentials, the relationship that will develop is extremely important. In that first visit, keep in mind always that this is the person upon whom your life—or that of a loved one—might someday depend. Does this doctor take the time to listen to and answer your questions or does he or she rush patients through the office on an assembly-line basis? Above all, do you *like* this doctor and feel confident in his or her hands?

The way a doctor touches his or her patient, with sureness and gentleness, is usually a strong indication of a genuinely caring instinct (or, through touch, the exact opposite in his or her personality can be sensed). The prospective patient should also be wary of the physician who relies exclusively on X rays and hardly ever touches the patient. Much useful information can be quickly and easily obtained by a skilled doctor through the sense of touch—by tapping on the chest or the back as the patient inhales and exhales, by feeling the joints, by palpating the main arterial pulses and the veins, and by tactile examination of the abdomen, breasts, or genitalia.

Confidence in a doctor's ability is perhaps the most important ingredient in the doctor-patient relationship. Without it, a great deal—if not all—is lost. But it is equally important to *your* well-being that a doctor gives you the freedom to ask any and all the questions you may have. Kindness, patience, and an understanding of each patient's individual case is his or her just due. While none of these qualities directly reflects on the doctor's knowledge or expertise and his or her ability to diagnose or treat illness, their lack can create an unhappy and confused patient. This, in turn, can help to nullify the good feelings of any successful treatment administered. Thus, the best doctors know the vital importance of their patient's mental approach to the healing process.

All this is just as pertinent as the fact that the doctor has earned his or her diploma. In fact, more and more medical schools and examining boards are now recognizing the additional importance of the doctor's purely human qualities. Examiners who certify the competence of physicians are now extending their assessments beyond demonstrable knowledge and technical proficiency to include estimates of the depth of the doctor's concern for human welfare. In most cases, "board certified" may also mean the same genuine caring of the midnight horse-and-buggy house calls of past generations. Even in a seemingly impersonal computerized era, human skill and a caring spirit are still the basis of good medicine. Your doctor should have both.

But doctors are not superhuman; they are ordinary people but usually with a genuine desire to help others through the application of their special talents. They have the same weaknesses and strengths we all have and are subject to the same illnesses. In addition, owing to long, demanding work hours and constant exposure to the crises of other people, their family relationships are often more strained than those of the average person whose sleep is never disturbed by emergency calls and who doesn't worry over critically ill patients. Doctors, furthermore, face the occupational hazard of easy-to-obtain drugs and, as does everyone else, alcohol. If you suspect that the doctor in whose care you have placed yourself is impaired, there are discreet ways to verify your suspicions. County and state medical societies usually have "impairment committees" whose job it is to determine and discover impaired physicians. In any case, if you are beginning to feel uneasy about your doctor, it's probably time for a change.

People who live in or close to large urban centers—New York, Boston, Chicago, Los Angeles, Philadelphia—have a wide choice of nationally recognized physicians specializing in the advanced treatment of certain conditions and working in some of the best equipped hospitals in the world. In succeeding chapters we have furnished lists for both you and your doctor of those hospitals and of some of the doctors who have helped to make them famous. Your own doctor, if well chosen, is there to help you make those important health care decisions as well as to refer you to the more highly specialized treatment available.

Whomever you have chosen, though, and however dire his or her diagnosis of your particular illness, keep in mind Norman Cousins, former editor of the *Saturday Review of Literature*. In 1964, having refused to accept as final the combined medical prognosis of a potentially fatal and irreversible collagen illness of his body's connective tissues, Cousins moved out of the hospital to a nearby hotel and set about curing himself with laughter. He had his nurses read humorous books to him, and he watched old Marx Brothers movies and reruns of *Candid Camera*. To his doctors' amazement, he recovered. In 1978 the prestigious *New England Journal of Medicine* printed Cousins' article, "The Anatomy of an Illness," which later became a best-selling book. As a result, the ex-editor became a researcher in the biochemistry of emotions and a professor of medical humanities at the UCLA School of Medicine. At 74, he still plays golf and tennis. His message: Help your doctor help you by keeping a positive, upbeat attitude; your doctor can't do the job alone.

· 2 ·
CHOOSING THE BEST
HOSPITALS AND CLINICS

Time was—and a very short time ago indeed—when few Americans had ever thought about or even heard of a teaching hospital. Some people still believe it is a place where young medical college graduates are allowed to practice on unsuspecting patients. The local hospital, usually large and imposing, was where your family doctor sent you when the need arose, and you unquestioningly went.

After World War II, the quietly prestigious teaching hospitals affiliated with almost every major college and university throughout the United States began to grow by leaps and bounds. With the wartime advent of penicillin, blood plasma, and the other medical marvels emanating from university research laboratories, these institutions attracted to their staffs the most brilliant and experienced young doctors—many of whom served in the war and therefore knew how to administer these discoveries as well as how to teach others about them.

These teaching institutions expanded into the great medical centers of today, available to all and encompassing every branch of medicine and surgery. But perhaps their greatest legacy is the practice and maintenance of the highest possible medical standards in the world.

We are not suggesting, however, that you (or a family member) appear on the doorstep of a medical center to be admitted for treatment. Except in emergencies, hospitals usually require a referral from a physician before a patient may be admitted. Of course, if you are fortunate enough to live near a city with a teaching hospital, and if your own doctor is a staff member, then your admission is made easy. Or you can always make an appointment with any of the doctors who are a part of these teaching, research, or clinical facilities to arrange an examination and consultation.

In the face of soaring health care costs, you should know that most of the university-affiliated hospitals are doing their utmost through special administrative committees to provide patients on an individual basis with payment plans utilizing personal and group health insurance. Except for the expense that may be incurred by long-distance air or ground transportation (either from your home to the hospital or from one hospital to another), the costs of medical care are usually no more in the teaching centers than in many privately run hospitals. Also, it is often the medical professors and department heads (on salary) who will perform a necessary operation at a somewhat lower fee than that of a high-priced, independent surgeon at a community hospital.

Although the smaller accredited hospitals and clinics are usually quite adequate for uncomplicated illnesses, more and more local doctors today prefer to send their seriously ill and hard-to-manage patients to a carefully chosen medical center. "It is better, after all," said one doctor, "to lose temporary control of a patient while there is still time for a possible cure than to lose him altogether."

From the patient's point of view, the following five considerations should be kept in mind when choosing a hospital.

1. The teaching centers have the latest diagnostic tools.
2. They have the trained surgical-medical teams who have worked together many times and know how to handle any situation that may arise from your illness.
3. They have the most experienced surgeons, based on the number of patients treated annually.
4. They are academic in motivation, no matter who the patient may be.
5. They receive state and federal grants, which help to offset the costs of patient care.

The transition from a personal-care physician to a higher medical authority is not always an easy one. If, for some reason (such as false pride, hurt feelings, or the desire for more time or tests), your doctor is reluctant to help you change your medical management, it may be time to ask him or her what is perhaps the most important question of all: *"Where would you go, doctor, for the best medical care if you or a member of your family were in the same position?"* The answer—as the doctor knows better than most—may well save your life. When you have decided, on the basis of your doctor's knowledge and your own research, where the best treatment can be found, ask your doctor to arrange the referral. He or she will then continue to feel a part of the team effort to help you. Also, depending on each individual's needs, it may be difficult to obtain the necessary care without your doctor's help in the prompt delivery of your records.

Ordinarily, most local doctors—in view of the many difficult medical problems encountered today—are only too glad to learn by continuing to follow, even remotely, the progress of a patient in the hands of a more qualified physician. Bitterness, belligerence, and uncooperative behavior, however, must be dealt with firmly in writing. Briefly and clearly stated, your note should repeat your decision to find other medical care and should ask your doctor to forward, as soon as possible, *legible* copies of your records, lab test results, and other special studies to the doctor, hospital, or clinic where you will be continuing your treatment. Because some original materials must be sent (X rays usually should not be copied), assure your doctor that they will be safely returned to him or her along with any information about further work being done. If there is still difficulty in obtaining the records and achieving cooperation, you may decide to call on the county medical society with which your doctor is associated to help in the matter.

It is desirable, of course, to have hospital medical care near one's home, family, and friends, but this may not be best for the patient in search of the most successful treatment. Those who live in or near a large city, for instance, may be told, "You don't have to leave Pittsburgh; we have everything you need right here." In these times of ultraspecialization, however, Boston, Houston, Rochester, or New York City may have better facilities for the patient involved.

The modern patient must be prepared to travel—perhaps a considerable distance—to achieve the best care and treatment for his or her particular medical problem. Fortunately, air transportation is keeping pace with the nation's medical needs, and ambulance planes are becoming widely available. Some are even equipped to transport patients from an intensive-care unit in a local hospital to a unit in another hospital in another state with trained medical personnel overseeing the journey. (See Chapter 15.) Also, special travel arrangements for ill people can be made with commercial airlines. We should point out that some insurance policies shoulder a generous share of such transportation costs, and Medicare will cover costs "for limited travel to the nearest place where necessary care is available."

Although expenses are not usually a factor for most people when a life may be at stake, it is comforting to know in advance that some major medical health care plans cover the costs of expensive or prolonged treatment. There are also third-party insurers, such as the corporation for whom you may work; employers are becoming more and more active in the field of employee health insurance. Keep in mind that most medical institutions of high standing have sophisticated social service departments able to help the less well-off meet their medical bills through adapted time payment plans.

For the study and treatment of some diseases, there are grants available that may be used to defray the cost of the treatments given in many teaching institutions. The better medical centers, furthermore, have built-in clinics which, for a reasonable fee, provide patients with access to the very same medical expertise available to private patients. Thus, patients of modest means should not be discouraged from seeking out superior medical care centers and traveling to them if and when necessary.

It should be stressed here that although the ability to pay top fees may have some bearing on the availability of second-best care, it is never true of the very best medical talent and reputation. Nor does possession of an abundance of money automatically guarantee the best medical care. Instead, it is up to the individual who is ill (or to his or her spokesperson) to determine the quality of medical care to seek with the funds available to him or her. With very few exceptions, the cost of hospital care is about the same everywhere—that is to say, very high. So when the need is great and the time is short, why not choose the best medical care and talent available?

THE 25 BEST MEDICAL CENTERS IN THE UNITED STATES

The major hospitals and medical centers have largely achieved their status because they pool the input of the many expert technicians and specialists on their staffs. The doctor in charge of the particular procedure has at his or her fingertips all the information he or she needs to know from all departments. But the "super hospitals"—meaning those judged as being the very best by a majority of medical professionals—have the added distinction of housing the innovators and pioneers of today's far-reaching research programs. Periodic surveys made among leading physicians, administrators, scientists, and lab researchers have shown, in fact, that the best hospitals remain the best—the only real difference over the years is in the growing number of institutions now labeled "best."

A great many hospitals with strong expertise in only a few departments are named throughout the book on our lists of doctor-recommended medical centers to go to for treatment in certain specialties. But the entries on our list of the 25 best hospitals in the United States all scored strong in at least eight departments in general medicine and surgery. They are listed here along with short summaries of their particular areas of expertise. The reader should remember that a center's exact position on the list is less important than the fact that these are peer institutions, with differences often reflected in the particular emphasis given to certain aspects of a specialty.

1. Mayo Graduate School of Medicine—Mayo Clinic
   200 S. W. First Street
   Rochester, MN 55905
   (507) 284-2511

With expenditures nearly paralleling those of the government-based National Institutes of Health, the Mayo Clinic provides facilities for about 900 physicians and scientists to research virtually every area of human disease. Mayo cancer research is currently emphasizing intraoperative radiation, which enables the surgeon to focus X rays directly upon exposed tumors while sparing the surrounding normal tissues; and their cardiology research is developing new, more effective drugs to help heart-attack patients. The clinic was one of the first centers in the United States to possess the German-devised litho-tripter, which uses sound waves to fragment some types of kidney stones and gallstones. The cochlear implant, enabling certain nerve-deaf patients to hear noises, and even some speech, is also achieving much success here. Liver transplant operations are well under way, directly by the noted physician Dr. Ruud Krom, formerly of the Netherlands. Two satellite clinics, staffed by Mayo personnel, are operating in Jacksonville, Florida, and Scottsdale, Arizona, to serve patients in those areas. The Mayo Graduate School of Medicine is a degree-granting institution.

2. Massachusetts General Hospital
   32 Fruit Street
   Boston, MA 02114
   (617) 726-2000

"Mass. General," the largest hospital in New England, is a primary teaching center for Harvard University Medical School and has a long tradition of pioneering research and treatment in numerous medical and surgical specialties. It continues to be noted for its outstanding work in cardiology; current research focuses on a partial artificial heart, which substitutes a prosthesis for only the damaged section(s)—this is expected to be suitable for many more patients than the somewhat cumbersome Jarvik-7 artificial heart. The treatment of severe burns took great strides here, in collaboration with the Massachusetts Institute of Technology, with the development of artificial skin, while human skin transplants are made possible by the laboratory culture of skin cells. At this hospital in 1962 occurred the first successful reattachment of a severed human limb by Dr. Ronald A. Malt, then a resident and now the chief of gastroenterological surgery. Extensive work on monoclonal antibodies has important applications for the treatment of heart disease, kidney disease, cancer, and Alzheimer's disease. The Stroke Center at Massachusetts General is known for its results in promoting advanced degrees of recovery.

3. University of Alabama Medical Center
   619 South 19th Street-University Station
   Birmingham, AL 35294
   (205) 934-4011

This medical complex, with its many strong departments in medicine and surgery, has an annual research budget of over $60 million. Some of its current programs include critical-care cancer treatment and the genetic cloning of tumor-specific antibodies as an aid to the diagnosis and treatment of cancer. Important research is also taking place in the field of nuclear cardiology, a subspecialty of radiology and nuclear medicine. Nuclear cardiology entails the injection of radioactive isotopes into the bloodstream so that the blood supply to the heart can be estimated; for example, the red blood cells can be tagged with a radioactive substance such as thallium, and the output of the heart can thus be measured before and after exercise. The University of Alabama had one of the first arthritis rehabilitation centers in the country and is also noted for its expertise in hand surgery and spinal cord injuries. A national toll-free telephone service that furnishes local doctors with needed information on a host of medical topics is unique in the nation, as is the critical-care transportation unit (see page 204).

4. Johns Hopkins Hospital
   600 North Wolfe Street
   Baltimore, MD 21205
   (301) 955-5000

Under the umbrella name of the Johns Hopkins Medical Institutions, the hospital, the Johns Hopkins Medical School, and the Johns Hopkins Medical and Surgical Association form a giant medical complex. The newest addition, in 1982, is the $42-million Adolph Meyer Center for the Neurosciences and Psychiatry—a medical center "first," which brings the departments of psychiatry, neurology, and neurosurgery under one roof. Johns Hopkins is also the developer of the automatic implantable defibrillator for the prevention of sudden death from cardiac rhythm disturbances; this device cuts the death rate in half for patients who are subject to frequent cardiac arrest. The first total knee-joint replacement was also developed here. Johns Hopkins Hospital is a pioneer in many other research areas including plasmapheresis, which is a method of blood-cell cleansing in connection with the treatment of certain autoimmune disorders and cancer; the development of techniques for observing how nerves "talk" to each other, and the development of closed-chest heart massage, known the world over as CPR for the resuscitation of heart-attack victims, and credited with saving thousands of lives. In urology, Dr. Patrick Walsh's method of prostate gland removal, which preserves the nerves that are important for bladder control and sexual performance, is being widely adopted. The Wilmer Eye Institute has few equals in the world.

5. Baylor College of Medicine and Hospitals
   One Baylor Plaza
   Houston, TX 77030
   (713) 798-4951

With eight hospitals in its own group, Baylor is itself a part of the Texas Medical Center at Houston. It is perhaps most famous for the pioneering heart surgery of Dr. Michael DeBakey. Patients come to Baylor from many areas of the world for difficult operations in the fields of cardiothoracic and gastrointestinal surgery. In the Influenza Research Center, Baylor scientists are currently at work developing new drugs such as Ribivarin that prevents various strains of flu. Its Children's Nutrition Research Center has a unique program of nutrition for pregnant women who anticipate breast-feeding their infants and for mothers who are in the process of breast-feeding. Geneticists and cell biologists are experimenting with the cloning of normal genes to replace defective ones, and Baylor is also in the forefront of centers that perform prenatal examinations of the human placenta to detect possible chromosomal abnormalities associated with Tay-Sachs, an inherited disease producing neurological abnormalities.

6. University of Washington Medical Center
   1959 N. E. Pacific Street
   Seattle, WA 98195
   (206) 548-3300

In the northwest corner of the medical map of the United States, the University of Washington Medical Center (including University Hospital and Harborview Medical Center) is a bulwark of science for the vast surrounding area as well as an important contributor to the state of American medicine. Forty percent of the patients checking into this hospital are from other parts of the country; many of them have been referred for specialized treatment at the Pain Center, the Spinal Cord Injury Center, the Prenatal Medicine Center, or the Cancer Center, which administers treatments with such sophisticated equipment as the cyclotron. Some outstanding research at the University of Washington includes: the Scribner Cannula, devised in 1960 by Dr. Belding Scribner, which makes long-term kidney dialysis possible; pioneer work on bone-marrow transplants for the treatment of some leukemias; and outstanding work on the causes of atherosclerosis (a form of arteriosclerosis) by Dr. Russell Ross, chairman of pathology, and Dr. John Glomset, biochemist. The departments of bioengineering and biological structure have contributed a special laser device, invented by Dr. Wylie Lee, for the treatment of some types of female infertility. The University of Washington also has its own Northwest Intensive Care Airlift for the transport of ill patients directly to the hospital.

7. Cleveland Clinic Foundation
   9500 Euclid Avenue
   Cleveland, OH 44106
   (216) 444-2200

Long famous for its expertise and research in the cardiovascular field, Cleveland Clinic is staffed by researchers who are now perfecting an arterial laser catheter that vaporizes the plaque material of clogged and narrowed blood vessels resulting from atherosclerosis. In addition to its well-known work in open-heart surgery, major programs include a comprehensive artificial-organ research department headed by the noted Japanese physician Dr. Yki Nose, and a major human organ center for transplants of hearts, heart-lung combinations, livers, kidneys, pancreases, corneas, and bone marrow. Although cardiothoracic cardiovascular research and surgery account for much of the clinic's worldwide reputation, it is also a major cancer treatment center and possesses an outstanding neurosensory center (with visual, hearing, and speech departments). It has a fine department for the treatment of muscular-skeletal disorders where current research focuses on materials to bond artificial components to bones, thus curtailing the need for hip and other joint replacement operations to repair the body's weakening structure.

8. Hospital of the University of Pennsylvania
   3400 Spruce Street
   Philadelphia, PA 19104
   (215) 662-4000

Established in 1874, the Hospital of the University of Pennsylvania was the first hospital to be owned by a medical school. It is famous as a tertiary-care center treating the most complex and critical conditions of patients. Besides offering the newest form of medical imaging—magnetic resonance imaging (MRI)—it has a wide range of specialized diagnostic services available to in-patients and to patients who use the diagnostic clinic. The Hospital of the University of Pennsylvania was a pioneer in the development of balloon angioplasty, a noninvasive method of dilating blocked arteries. It has also gained a wide reputation for the treatment of infertility problems, and new cosmetic-surgery techniques (especially those involving craniofacial reconstruction) continue to be developed in the nation's oldest department of plastic surgery. The cardiothoracic surgical unit is noted for its work on certain rhythmic disturbances of the heart; in certain cases, the damaged portion of the heart is peeled away, thus promoting normal rhythm and output. The Neurosurgery Unit is a center for the care of head injuries, and the Smell and Taste Center is one of a very few of its kind in the country. Closely associated academically is the famous Scheie Eye Institute, located at the nearby University of Pennsylvania–affiliated Presbyterian Hospital. Here, too, is the Wistar Institute, famous for its research in cancer, AIDS, and other diseases.

9. Duke University Medical Center
   Box 3005
   Durham, NC 27710
   (919) 684-5587

At his death in 1925, James Buchanan Duke left $4 million to build a medical school, a hospital, and a nurses' residence. Today the Duke complex has an annual budget of $346 million, a 1,008-bed hospital, and a distinguished faculty of 1,400 specialists and researchers. It is one of 20 federally funded comprehensive cancer centers with 195 cancer specialists, a 20-bed clinical research section, and an 8-bed bone-marrow transplant unit. Surgery for certain cardiac arrhythmias is well advanced, and the first operation to control Wolff-Parkinson-White syndrome, a rhythmic disturbance of the heart, was performed at Duke in 1968. The diagnostic radiology section is equipped with three magnetic resonance imaging (MRI) devices, a positron emission tomography (PET) unit, and a SPECT—single photon emission computer tomography—unit, all of which help to diagnose not only abnormal structures within the body but also the abnormal functioning of those structures. Forty diagnostic imaging rooms are variously equipped with ultrasound, nuclear imaging, and various scanning devices. Its ophthalmology department is well known throughout the world, as is its reputation for the treatment of immunodeficiency diseases and its successful use of half-matched bone-marrow transplants, especially in the treatment of very young children.

10. University of California San Francisco Hospitals and Clinics
    505 Parnassus Avenue
    San Francisco, CA 94143
    (415) 476-1000

The University of California San Francisco is an internationally recognized center for biomedical research. The Schools of Medicine and Pharmacy receive more research monies from the National Institutes of Health than any of their peer institutions throughout the country. Because of the close interaction between basic and clinical scientists, the patient receives the latest in research benefits. It was in 1953 that a UCSF biochemist teamed with a Stanford scientist to develop the original DNA technology that has since blossomed into the whole field of genetic engineering. Clinicians and basic scientists are working together with oral-cancer specialists from the School of Dentistry and are presently launching a major attack on AIDS. Among the many other innovations being advanced here is the perfecting of the cochlear ear implant—a multi-channel device to provide speech recognition to the deaf. Basic research at UCSF is presently focused on cancer-causing genes called *oncogenes* and on the investigation into the role of an infectious agent—the prion—as the cause of such neurological disorders as Alzheimer's disease. Care of the elderly is emphasized in the School of Nursing, and in the Cardiovascular Institute at UCSF, the new science of neonatology—the treatment of newborns—had much of its beginning.

11. New York Hospital–Cornell Medical Center
    525 East 68th Street
    New York, NY 10021
    (212) 746-5454

This institution stands at the center of the world's leading private biomedical complex. Sharing faculty, students, and staff, it is cooperatively associated in research and patient care with the Memorial Sloan-Kettering Cancer Center, Rockefeller University, and the Hospital for Special Surgery. Its high-risk pregnancy program is the most advanced in the New York area, and it has a new pediatric intensive-care unit as well as a new recreational center for young patients. It is one of a handful of centers in the country to be designated by the National Institutes of Health as a research center for burn injury, and its Department of Rehabilitation Medicine has developed new methods of minimizing scar formation in serious facial burns. It is also one of less than a dozen centers to be designated by the same organization as a Specialized Center of Research (SCOR) in hypertension. New York–Cornell's radiology department was the first in the area (indeed, one of the first in the country) to pioneer magnetic resonance imaging (MRI), and the new Stitch Radiation Therapy

Center has been designed to be cooperatively used with the Memorial Sloan-Kettering Cancer Center. The department of anesthesiology has a Nerve Block Clinic for relief of many kinds of pain. New York–Cornell is also one of four centers testing a new portable kidney dialysis machine that works while the victim of kidney disease pursues his or her normal activities. Its ophthalmology and neurology departments are among the leaders in research and patient care in these specialties.

12. University of Michigan Hospitals
    1500 East Medical Center Drive
    Ann Arbor, MI 48109
    (313) 936-4000

University of Michigan Hospitals include the Ambulatory Care Services, Main Hospital, C. S. Mott Children's Hospitals, Women's Hospital, Holden Prenatal Hospital, the Adult Psychiatric Hospital, the Children's and Adolescents' Psychiatric Hospital, and the W. K. Kellogg Eye Center. The depth and breadth of its facilities for clinical and research programs in every medical and surgical specialty makes it one of the most versatile medical centers in the United States. Its major research laboratories concentrate on allergy, gastroenterology, endocrinology, hearing (including cochlear implants), hypertension, and neuroscience. Special imaging facilities include magnetic resonance imaging (MRI), positron emission tomography (PET), a cyclotron, and digital subtraction coronary angiography, which can automatically give a doctor information about the thickness of blood vessel walls. The radiation-therapy computerized treatment planning system is one of the most sophisticated systems in the nation. The University of Michigan has a National Institutes of Health–supported Clinical Research Center and a unit of the Howard Hughes Medical Research Institute with a core group in molecular genetics. The Medical Scientist Training Program is providing medical students with doctoral research capabilities, and graduates earn both M.D. and Ph.D. degrees.

13. Brigham and Women's Hospital
    75 Francis Street
    Boston, MA 02115
    (617) 732-5500

The name and style of this outstanding medical center derives from the merger several years ago of two Harvard-affiliated hospitals: the Boston Lying-In Hospital, and the Peter Bent Brigham Hospital, where in the mid-1950s the first successful human kidney transplant was performed. Research at Brigham and Women's still continues on such allied topics as tissue compatibility and various immunosuppressive mechanisms and drugs. Topping the list of other strong departments are those of cardiothoracic surgery and cardiology, plastic and reconstructive surgery, urology, obstetrics and gynecology, internal medicine, and neoperinatal medicine. In fact, modern medicine and surgery owe much of their present-day expertise to the kind of teaching that characterizes this medical center. Although there is continuing emphasis on patient care and welfare, its physicians and surgeons historically were among the first to show that there is nothing incompatible with strong teaching programs, basic and clinical research, and good care for patients.

14. Yale–New Haven Hospital
    333 Cedar Street
    New Haven, CT 06510
    (203) 785-4242

Yale University's College of Medicine, with its affiliated teaching hospital, has long been a center of medical scholarship. One of the pioneers in fetus-in-utero research, the center is also famous for the work in fetal cardiology of Dr. John Hobbins and Dr. Charles Kleinman. Dr. Marvin Sears of the Ophthalmology Department and a team of researchers developed Timoptic, an important drug for the treatment of glaucoma. The New Haven Hospital's Newborn Special Care Unit, established in 1962, was one of the first such centers in the world. Methotrexate and other anticancer drugs have evolved from the work of Yale's Pharmacology Department, while the work in chemotherapy, particularly for cancers of the head and neck, is well known to referring doctors. Current work includes a new technology for the treatment of epilepsy and further advances in the treatment of Hodgkin's disease.

15. Vanderbilt University Medical Center
    1211 22nd Avenue South
    Nashville, TN 37232
    (615) 322-7311

Although Vanderbilt has a wide range of clinical research departments, it is especially famous for several outstanding programs, including the medical and surgical treatment of kidney diseases (Vanderbilt ranks seventh in the world for kidney transplant operations) and diabetology. Expertise in these two fields led in 1985 to the development of another: a pancreas transplant program. This addition places Vanderbilt as one of the top hospitals in the nation for all types of transplant operations. Its Center for Fertility and Reproductive Research (C-FARR) features an outstanding male infertility test center and in-vitro fertilization capabilities—the center's pregnancy rate for all childless couples studied and treated there is 60 percent. The Center for Research on the Epidermal Growth Factor is directed by Dr. Stanley Cohen, professor of biochemistry, whose isolation of EGF and subsequent study of how it makes cells grow is internationally recognized as having great potential for the advancement of cancer research. The development of an antivenin against the bite of the brown recluse spider and of a medicine that greatly reduces tissue damage from such bites are other noteworthy discoveries.

16. University of Miami Affiliated Hospitals
    1475 N. W. 12th Avenue
    Miami, FL 33136
    (305) 547-6418

This university's medical college and hospitals (including the Jackson Memorial Hospital and the world-famous Bascom Palmer Eye Institute) have an international reputation as research centers in several medical fields. It is one of the largest medical centers in this country and contains one of the few centers for blood diseases in the field of hematology. Among the University of Miami's medical advances are the transplanting of the islets of Langerhans (the areas of the pancreas that normally supply the blood with insulin) in severe cases of diabetes, the surgical replacement of a diseased bladder with an artificial organ developed by the department of urology, and the treatment at Dr. Hubert Rosomoff's Comprehensive Pain Center of chronic back pain through a four-week course of grueling exercise, psychological counseling, and vocational guidelines. After treating 7,000 patients, the clinic claims a success rate of 86 percent; "success" in this case means a return to normalcy, although usually not without some pain. In addition, Miami's National Parkinson's Foundation (see page 156), backed by the Neurology Department of the university, is outstanding in its field.

17. University of Minnesota Hospitals
    Harvard Street at East River Road
    Minneapolis, MN 55455
    (612) 626-3000

The University of Minnesota is recognized as the leading organ transplant center in the world. Most types of organ transplants are done here, including pancreas transplants for advanced diabetic patients and bone-marrow transplants for certain leukemias. It is also well known for the quality of its research and treatment of cardiovascular diseases. The world's first open-heart surgery was performed here in 1954, and Minnesota pioneered the use of the heart-lung machine for such surgery. The University of Minnesota's treatment for cancer is highly sophisticated and includes the Thermatron RF, a Japanese-built hyperthermia machine that destroys tumors through the use of low-frequency radio waves. Cancer researcher Dr. Jorge Yunis has developed a test that helps to identify persons who are cancer prone through the study of weak spots in their chromosomes. The dietary influence of high-potassium low-salt foods on arterial walls is an important area of research in strokes and heart attacks; it has been shown by Minnesota researchers Dr. Louis Tobian that a high-potassium diet "affords remarkable protection against death from strokes as well as against kidney damage."

18. University of Texas–Southwestern Medical Center
    5323 Harry Hines Boulevard
    Dallas, TX 75235
    (214) 688-3111

The principal affiliated teaching hospital is:

Parkland Memorial Hospital
5201 Harry Hines Boulevard
Dallas, TX 75235
(214) 590-8011

Affiliated with Southwestern Graduate School of Biomedical Sciences, this center is the most comprehensive division of the University of Texas's medical center system. Through the outstanding faculty they have attracted, Texas-Southwestern has risen to the front rank of world medical centers. Emphasis is placed upon the scientific basis of medical practice. The number and quality of its basic research and clinical programs, which offer superior care for patients with a variety of disorders, are outstanding. For example, the center is famous for the treatment of burn victims, especially its Intensive Burn Care Unit for Children. It has the world's largest bankable organ and tissue bank for corneas, bones, skin, and other transplants. It is also recognized as a leading center in the world for research on the molecular basis of cholesterol metabolism as applied to the treatment of arteriosclerotic heart disease and gallstones. Two faculty members (Drs. Jonathan Uhr and Ellen Vitetta) have won top awards for demonstrating that a far-advanced tumor in a patient could be successfully treated by the use of immunotoxins. Texas-Southwestern has been a pioneer in developing high-field magnetic resonance imaging for clinical diagnosis, and besides being noted for basic and clinical cardiology, this center is known for its work in mineral metabolism and the prevention of kidney stones. This relatively new medical school has had three Nobel laureates.

19. Northwestern University Medical Center
    250 East Superior Street
    Chicago, IL 60611
    (312) 649-2000

Included in this outstanding midwestern medical center are Memorial Hospital and Children's Hospital in Chicago, and Evanston Hospital. Two new departments of cell biology and molecular biology are applying basic research to the treatment of a variety of diseases. Its Multiple Purpose Arthritis Center, funded by the National Institutes of Health, is one of only 14 such centers in the country, and it also has a center for childhood arthritis. The Rehabilitation Engineering Program includes joint replacement, prosthetics, and totally barrier-free environment for paraplegics. The versatile neurology department includes the Les Turner Foundation for the study of amyotrophic lateral sclerosis (ALS), also known as Lou Gehrig's disease. The Institute of Psychiatry at Northwestern has an outstanding alcohol and drug abuse program, specializing in the treatment of professional athletes. The obstetrics and gynecology department particularly at the Evanston division, has long been one of the best in the nation; its center for multiple births and the associated risks is unique. Laser surgery is highly developed at Northwestern in a number of departments: otolaryngology, dermatology (with a dye laser for the removal of unsightly birthmarks), ophthalmology, and especially neurosurgery.

20. Barnes Hospital
    One Barnes Plaza
    St. Louis, MO 63110
    (314) 362-5000

Barnes is the principal teaching hospital associated with Washington University. It is a regional trauma center for Missouri and Illinois and is well known as a center for the medical and surgical care of heart diseases, performing over 2,500 heart operations annually. Surgical areas of particular expertise at Barnes include ophthalmology, otolaryngology, plastic and reconstructive surgery, and urology. It was one of the first hospitals in the United States to test tissue plasminogen activator (t-PA), which dissolves blood clots that can cause heart attacks. Barnes was one of the first centers in the world to treat diabetics through the use of insulin (in 1920); today's researchers there are involved with transplanting the islets of Langerhans, the insulin-producing structures of the pancreas; this operation may someday relieve diabetics of their dependence upon insulin. Percutaneous removal of some kidney stones avoids more extensive surgery, and Barnes now has a litho-tripter for crushing kidney stones with shock waves. The Mallinckrodt Institute of Radiology at Barnes is another world leader in almost all types of radiology research and technology, including the use of CAT, PET, and MRI scanners, facilitating the diagnosis of many diseases. Along with its surgical and chemotherapy programs, the availability of these scanners places this hospital in the forefront of cancer treatment centers.

21. University of Pittsburgh Medical and Health Care Division
    3811 O'Hara Street
    Pittsburgh, PA 15213
    (412) 624-3530

The University of Pittsburgh Medical and Health Care Division includes the most highly regarded liver transplant center in the country, directed by Dr. Thomas Starzl. Outstanding also as a cancer treatment center, Pittsburgh deserves top honors in the field of breast cancer treatment owing to the monumental work of Dr. Bernard Fisher, who in 1985 published the results of the largest prospective comparative study of historical and current methods of treating this disease. Another outstanding department is the Western Psychiatric Institute, directed by Dr. David Kupfer and known for its work on depression. The Children's Hospital is unexcelled for the treatment of ear disease, and the center is also the home of the Institute of Plastic and Reconstructive Surgery. The dermatology department, headed by Dr. Brian Jegasothy, specializes in the diagnosis of rare skin diseases. Dr. Mark May of the otolaryngology department is well known for operations to repair facial nerve paralysis. It is now the world's leading center for the treatment of cranial base tumors.

22. University of Colorado Health Sciences Center
    4200 East Ninth Avenue
    Denver, CO 80262
    (303) 329-3066

At this versatile medical center, the first liver transplant operations in the United States were performed over fifteen years ago. A new heart transplant program now is in progress, while the center continues its work with kidney transplants. Basic research into the genetics of cancer under the direction of Dr. Theodore Puck is a strong program at the center's famed Eleanor Roosevelt Cancer Research Institute. The Barbara Davis Institute for Childhood Diabetes is one of the University of Colorado's many pediatric institutions, including the Rocky Mountain Center for Childhood Development. Dr. Alden Harken, chief of surgery, and his associates are studying arrhythmic hearts and the appropriate surgery for such cases. Other areas of outstanding expertise are studies into the sleep patterns of adults and children, multiple sclerosis research, and a unique geriatric-care clinical services department.

23. Stanford University Medical Center
    300 Pasteur Drive
    Stanford, CA 94305
    (415) 723-4000

Scientific advances have given Stanford Medical Center its reputation as one of the world's outstanding research centers. It has a unique combination of scientists in basic and clinical research who are involved in day-to-day patient care. Both groups are collaborating to bring laboratory advances to patients as rapidly as possible. The first human heart transplant in the United States was done here in 1968, as well as the world's first successful combined heart-lung transplant in 1981. Stanford was responsible also, in 1957, for the first use in the Western Hemisphere of the linear accelerator to treat cancer. Careful research by the late Dr. Henry Kaplan, professor of radiology, and Dr. Saul Rosenberg, professor of oncology, into Hodgkin's disease (a form of cancer of the lymphatic system) changed the outlook from fatal in almost all cases to an 80 percent permanent cure of this disease. Human genetic research at Stanford is already yielding practical results since the report of the first successful use of monoclonal antibodies (1981) to treat cancer. Application of new technology to the area of newborn intensive care at Stanford has resulted in the survival of about 75 percent of infants weighing between 1.6 and 2.2 pounds at birth. Research into the physiology of sleep disorders and brain chemistry are two other areas of expertise at this institution.

24. Columbia-Presbyterian Medical Center
    622 West 168th Street
    New York, NY 10032
    (212) 305-2500

Associated with Columbia University's College of Physicians and Surgeons (one of five outstanding medical schools in New York City), Presbyterian Hospital is the principal center of Columbia University for research (basic and clinical) and patient care at all levels. It is one of only 21 centers in the country designated by the federal government as a comprehensive cancer center. Basic research in tumor markers, blood tests for cancer, and innovative treatment of cancer (mostly on an outpatient basis) continues to improve the outlook for patients with various types of malignant tumors. Dr. Sadek Hilal, a radiologist, pioneered the development of magnetic resonance imaging (MRI), one of the newest diagnostic techniques, which does not expose the patient to ionizing radiation. Application of basic research into the causes, treatment, and prevention of heart disease and strokes is far advanced at this center. It is one of 18 centers in the country regularly engaged in heart transplant operations. Laser surgery for a variety of eye conditions is one of the interests of its versatile department of ophthalmology, and its many laboratories are contributing to the advanced knowledge of genetic diseases, mechanisms of brain action, and nutrition, among numerous other subjects. Columbia-Presbyterian is also a center for fertility studies and in-vitro fertilization.

25. University of California Los Angeles Medical Center
    10833 Le Conte Avenue
    Los Angeles, CA 90024
    (213) 825-4321

UCLA is well known for its comprehensive care services and for a number of outstanding departments. The surgical services, under Dr. William P. Longmire, one of America's most versatile teachers and practitioners of surgery, are among the best in the world, and since the development of cyclosporin, the center has resumed its liver transplant program in addition to starting a heart transplant section. Equally famous are its Brain Research Center, Neurological Research Center, the Jules Stein Eye Institute, the Jerry Lewis Muscular Dystrophy Research facility, and the Neuropsychiatric Institute. Also of interest is the invention of a detachable balloon occluder by Dr. Grant Hieshima to close off bleeding vessels within the brain. The tiny balloon, guided by computerized imaging techniques, is threaded through the arterial network to just the right spot on the bleeding vessel. There it is inflated and left permanently. This method is safer and less expensive in selected cases than invasive surgical methods.

In addition to these hospitals, mention must be made of the National Institutes of Health (NIH), located in Bethesda, Maryland. NIH is an agency of the United States Department of Health and Human Services. It is one of the most comprehensive biomedical research centers in the world, housing hundreds of research laboratories, the 540-bed Warren Grant Magnuson Clinical Center, and the National Library of Medicine—the world's largest medical library. Among its 17 institutes and research divisions are the National Cancer Institute; the

National Eye Institute; the National Heart, Lung, and Blood Institute; the National Institute of Allergy and Infectious Diseases; the National Institute of Arthritis, Diabetes, and Digestive and Kidney Diseases; the National Institute of Child Health and Human Development; the National Institute of Dental Research; the National Institute of Environmental Health Sciences; the National Institute of Neurological and Communicative Disorders and Stroke; and the National Institute on Aging. Altogether, these institutes employ more than 15,000 people, of whom 3,000 have doctoral degrees and impressive records of accomplishment. Approximately 125 have won national and international awards and, since 1968, four staff members have received Nobel Prizes. In addition to its own activities, NIH supports research programs in numerous hospitals and universities both here and abroad.

Given certain conditions, anyone may be accepted at NIH for the diagnosis and treatment of medical problems. A patient must be recommended to NIH by his or her personal physician, with the essential information about the patient's condition given in writing. If the disease or disorder is one that is, or is about to be, the subject of an NIH-sponsored research program and if the prospective patient meets the requirements of such a program, he or she may then be accepted for treatment. Patients who have an obscure disease or one that has been unresponsive to treatment should have no hesitancy in asking their personal physicians to inquire about the possibility of consultation and/or treatment at NIH. Patients who are admitted to the NIH clinical facility for treatment are accepted without any charge. If it is unable to accept a patient at Bethesda, NIH will know of work taking place in the given field at NIH-funded private institutions.

One final note: patients who qualify for treatment in an NIH clinical research program should not harbor any idea that they are guinea pigs. No treatment will be given without the patient's informed consent, and no medicines will be administered that have not been completely tested for safety. For the staff of NIH, as with all good doctors, the welfare of the patient takes precedence over research objectives.

If you wish to have your doctor contact NIH, the address is:

> National Institutes of Health
> 9000 Rockville Pike
> Bethesda, MD 20205
> (301) 496-4114

Also in a class by itself: the nonprofit City of Hope National Pilot Medical Center and Beckman Research Institute (located in Duarte, California, 25 miles east of Los Angeles) treats thousands of eligible patients each year free of charge. On 93 acres in the foothills of the San Gabriel mountains, City of Hope has 2,000 professionals, including doctors and technicians, available in 50 buildings, where research on cancer, AIDS, and other diseases is ongoing. The free health and medical care is funded by 500 City of Hope local chapters across the United States. For referral, ask your local doctor how and where to apply for eligibility.

THE SUPER CLINICS

Usually included in every discussion of the prestigious hospitals and medical centers across the country are these major diagnostic and treatment clinics:

The Lahey Clinic Foundation
41 Mall Road
Burlington, MA 01815
(617) 273-5100

The Alton Ochsner Medical Foundation
1516 Jefferson Highway
New Orleans, LA 70121
(504) 838-3000

These clinics offer an advantage over conventional hospitals: The skills, knowledge, and lab work available, plus the know-how of doctors practicing in every phase of medicine, focus the input of several hundred people on one patient. The result is inevitably a superthorough diagnosis.

In addition, there are an estimated 40 to 50 specialty clinics of equally high standing located from coast to coast. Among the better known of these are:

Memorial Sloan-Kettering Cancer
    Center
1275 York Avenue
New York, NY 10021
(212) 794-6707

Bascom Palmer Eye Institute
900 N. W. 17th Street
Miami, FL 33136
(305) 326-6111

M. D. Anderson Hospital and Tumor
    Institute
6723 Bertner Drive
Houston, TX 77030
(713) 792-6170

Wills Eye Hospital
Ninth and Walnut Streets
Philadelphia, PA 19107
(215) 928-3000

Scripps Clinic and Research Foundation
10666 North Torey Pines Road
La Jolla, CA 92037
(619) 455-9100

Scheie Eye Institute
51 North 39th Street
Philadelphia, PA 19104
(215) 662-4000

Joslin Diabetes Clinic
One Joslin Place
Boston, MA 02215
(617) 732-2400

Jules Stein Eye Institute
800 Westwood Plaza
Los Angeles, CA 90024
(213) 825-8556

Massachusetts Eye and Ear Infirmary
243 Charles Street
Boston, MA 02114
(617) 522-8100

Patricia Neal Stroke Center
1901 Clinch Avenue, S. W.
Knoxville, TN 37916
(615) 546-2811

Shea Clinic (for ear disorders and diseases)
6133 Poplar Pike at Ridgeway
Box 17987
Memphis, TN 38119
(901) 761-9720

· 3 ·

MEDICINE: THE NINE
SUBSPECIALTIES

Although the umbrella term *medicine* embraces all forms of medical and surgical diagnosis and treatment, it is used here to designate the nonsurgical specialty fields of medical practice. These fields are described in this chapter to provide patients with a background of information they should know about their illnesses. Each is accompanied by a list of the best hospital centers for treatment in each field according to the states where they are located.

The lists of best hospitals found throughout this book highlight areas of special expertise in certain hospitals and point to important ongoing research in others. Busy physicians are often hard-pressed to keep informed of the latest work that is going on throughout the medical community—even in their own specialty. From these carefully researched lists, however, it is our hope that your personal physician may, when necessary, receive some help in guiding you to the proper medical center and helping you to make the right decisions regarding particular treatments.

The names of doctors given for contact purposes in the lists are, for the most part, the program directors in each specialty. They may not be heads of departments or professors at the teaching institutions of which the hospitals are a part, but the program director is nevertheless the doctor who knows best the individual expertise possessed by each doctor and surgeon in his or her department.

Also, the learned professor or the titular head of a department may or may not be the best physician for a particular patient. He or she may have somewhat narrow interests as far as his or her own practice is concerned, in addition to administrative duties that occupy a fair portion of time. Hence, he or she is not always available to take on a heavy patient load.

Clearly the best interests of a patient are served by the recommendations of teams of good doctors. Although a superior doctor working apart from a team is much in demand, he or she often tends to become overworked, or his or her energies may become impaired for one reason or another. But the team approach of highly trained doctors, nurses, and medical technicians working together to solve a serious medical problem both protects against and compensates for any possible misjudgment on the part of one doctor.

It is wise to remember that because of the great volume of work done in a teaching hospital, unnecessary operations are not apt to be recommended, nor are unnecessary diagnostic studies and tests undertaken—a routine experience for patients in many hospitals today. Also, the experienced operating surgeon, with his or her trained surgical team, has probably done several hundred similar operations in a single year.

With that comforting thought in mind, then, here are nine diagnostic medical specialties and lists of recommended centers, hospitals, and clinics with a strong department in each.

ALLERGY IMMUNOLOGY

Probably the fastest-growing of the basic medical sciences, *immunology* (the study of the human immune system) and its sister science, *allergy* (hypersensitivity to environmental substances such as dust, pollens, chemicals, foods, medicines, temperatures, and so on), have enabled doctors to devise record numbers of treatments for human diseases and disorders. Since the deciphering of the genetic code, with its new DNA technology, advances have been so continuous that medical practitioners are hard put to keep up with them.

To name a few advances: Researchers have uncovered ways of activating certain immune cells to increase by 20 percent the five-year life span of early lung cancer patients; in reverse, drugs that suppress the immune system can now eliminate the need for insulin shots in some diabetic children and can successfully treat some case of rheumatoid arthritis; also, immunology researchers have discovered a promising malaria vaccine. Because the AIDS virus, for example, attacks and destroys a major cell of the immune system, much of the success in AIDS research is owing to the work of immunologists.

Comparable only to the most complex of human organs—the brain—the immune network of disease-fighting guardian cells within body tissues and the blood stream is waging constant warfare on germs, pollutants, foreign elements, and other cellular matter that do not belong in a healthy body. Like the brain, too, the immune system has the mysterious ability to remember and store information. Memory cells, circulating in the blood stream after an infection, are thus readying the system to launch an immediate attack against the return of the same bacterial invaders.

The following hospitals and institutions are in the vanguard of both research and clinical treatment of allergies and immunologic disorders. Some names and places of special note include: Dr. John Kappler of the National Jewish Center for Immunology and Respiratory Medicine, Denver; Dr. Anthony Fauci, AIDS research coordinator, National Institute of Health, Washington, D.C.; Dr.

Robert Gallo, National Cancer Institute; and Dr. Richard Johnston, Jr., University School of Medicine, Philadelphia. Others, whose extensive published work have formed the basis for significant advances in immunology, are Dr. Eric Gershwin, Dr. Stephen Nagy Jr., and Dr. Michael Klass, at the University of California, Davis Medical Center, and Dr. Sharad D. Deodhar in the field of cancer immunology at the Cleveland Clinic.

California

Scripps Clinic and Research Foundation
10666 North Torey Pines Road
La Jolla, CA 92037
(619) 455-9100
Program Directors: Dr. Ronald Simon
Dr. Donald Stevenson

Children's Hospital of Los Angeles
4650 Sunset Boulevard
Los Angeles, CA 90027
(213) 660-2450
Program Director: Dr. Joseph A. Church

University of California Davis Medical Center
2315 Stockton Boulevard
Sacramento, CA 95817
(916) 453-3096
Program Director: Dr. Eric Gershwin

Colorado

University of Colorado Health Sciences Center
4200 East Ninth Avenue
Denver, CO 80262
(303) 329-3066
Program Director: Dr. Henry Clayman

National Jewish Center for Immunology and Respiratory Diseases
1400 Jackson Street
Denver, CO 80206
(303) 388-4461
Program Director: Dr. Harold S. Nelson

Illinois

Rush-Presbyterian-St. Luke's Medical Center
1653 West Congress Parkway
Chicago, IL 60612
(312) 942-6554
Program Director: Dr. Howard J. Zeitz

Iowa

University of Iowa Hospitals and Clinics
650 Newton Road
Iowa City, Iowa 52242
(319) 356-2117
Program Director: Dr. Hal B. Richerson

Massachusetts

Children's Hospital
300 Longwood Avenue
Boston, MA 02115
(617) 735-6000
Program Director: Dr. Raif Geha

Massachusetts General Hospital
32 Fruit Street
Boston, MA 02114
(617) 726-2000
Program Director: Dr. Kurt Bloch

Michigan

University of Michigan Hospitals
1500 East Medical Center Drive
Ann Arbor, MI 48109
(313) 936-4000
Program Director: Dr. William Solomon

Minnesota

Mayo Clinic
200 S. W. First Street
Rochester, MN 55905
(507) 284-2511
Program Director: Dr. Richard G. Van Dellen

New York

Mt. Sinai Hospital
One Gustav Levy Place
New York, NY 10029
(212) 650-6500
Program Director: Dr. Joseph Hassett
(This hospital is especially noted for outstanding work
in the fields of AIDS, herpes simplex, and other
closely related subjects, researched by Dr. Mark
Taff and Dr. Frederic Siegal.)

Columbia-Presbyterian Medical Center
622 West 168th Street
New York, NY 10032
(212) 305-2500
Program Director: Dr. William Davis

North Carolina	Duke University Medical Center Box 2898 Durham, NC 27710 (919) 684-5587 Program Director: Dr. Rebecca Buckley
Ohio	Children's Hospital Medical Center Elland and Bethesda Avenues Cincinnati, OH 45229 (513) 559-4200 Program Director: Dr. Thomas J. Fischer
	University of Ohio Children's Hospital Division 700 Children's Drive Columbus, OH 43205 (614) 461-2138 Program Director: Dr. Charles Miller
Pennsylvania	Hospital of the University of Pennsylvania 3400 Spruce Street Philadelphia, PA 19104 (215) 662-2425 Program Director: Dr. Burton Zweiman
	Children's Hospital of Philadelphia 34th Street at Civic Center Boulevard Philadelphia, PA 19104 (215) 596-9100 Program Director: Dr. Steven Douglas
Tennessee	LeBonheur Children's Medical Center One Children's Plaza Memphis, TN 38103 (901) 522-9000 Program Director: Dr. Lloyd Crawford
	University of Tennessee Medical Center 956 Court Avenue Memphis, TN 38103 (901) 528-6663 Program Director: Dr. Tai-June Yoo
Texas	Baylor College of Medicine and Hospitals One Baylor Plaza Houston, TX 77030 (713) 798-4951 Program Director: Dr. William A. Shearer

Washington   University of Washington Medical Center
                          1959 N. E. Pacific Street
                          Seattle, WA 98195
                          (206) 543-3293
                          Program Director: Dr. Paul Van Arsdel, Jr.

Wisconsin   Medical College of Wisconsin
                          8700 West Wisconsin Avenue
                          Milwaukee, WI 53226
                          (414) 257-6095
                          Program Director: Dr. Jordan Fink

DERMATOLOGY
(See also chapter 4, "Surgery")

It is difficult to think of a single medical specialty that does not bear at some point on the science of skin diseases. It used to be said, only half in jest, that the work of the dermatologist was comparatively easy and comfortable because his or her patients "never die and never get well." Well, the truth is that they do die and they do get well. Skin diseases, while occasionally simple and easily treatable, can be among the most challenging and stubborn problems in all of medicine, calling for a great knowledge of the basic sciences as well as wide clinical experience in managing skin diseases of many different kinds and causes.

Four years of postgraduate training are now required for certification in this specialty, the first year of which must include advanced work and practical experience in the diagnosis and treatment of patients with a wide variety of diseases. Further work includes special studies of allergy and immunology as they relate to skin diseases; knowledge of the many different drugs that may cause or be used to treat skin diseases; familiarity with bacteriology, virology, parasitology, and mycology (the study of fungi); opportunities to view and review thousands of photographs of skin conditions and a vast number of microscopic preparations of healthy and diseased skin; the effect of various forms of light on the skin; skin manifestations of diseases which also affect internal organs of the body; occupational diseases of and thermal effects on the skin; and surgical treatment of certain skin problems. So important is a knowledge of skin pathology (how skin diseases develop and the courses they take) that about two dozen fully accredited residencies in the field of dermatopathology are now available in the United States.

Retin-A, a recently approved skin medication derived from vitamin A, which smoothes wrinkles and reduces deep facial lines, has been shown to be safe to use around the eyes, as reported by Dr. John Voorhees to the American Academy of Dermatology in 1988. Also, in a one-year, 10-center study, the medication appears to decrease the number of precancerous lesions of the skin and to alter the genetic program of a cell, whether aging or malignant, according to a report by Dr. Barbara Gilchrest of Boston University.

Centers noted for work in dermatology include the following:

Alabama   University of Alabama Medical Center
                             619 South 19th Street/University Station
                             Birmingham, AL 35294
                             (205) 934-4141
                             Program Director: Dr. W. Mitchell Sams, Jr.

California   Stanford University Medical Center
                             300 Pasteur Drive
                             Stanford, CA 94305
                             (415) 723-4000
                             Program Director: Dr. Eugene A. Bauer

Colorado   University of Colorado Health Sciences Center
                             4200 East Ninth Avenue
                             Denver, CO 80262
                             (303) 329-3066
                             Program Director: Dr. William Weston

Connecticut   Yale–New Haven Hospital
                             333 Cedar Street
                             New Haven, CT 06510
                             (203) 785-4242
                             Program Director: Dr. Richard L. Edelson

Florida   University of Miami—Jackson Memorial Hospital
                             P.O. Box 016250 (R-250)
                             Miami, FL 33101
                             (305) 325-7429
                             Program Director: Dr. William Eaglstein

Georgia   Emory University Hospital
                             1364 Clifton Road, N. E.
                             Atlanta, GA 30322
                             (404) 727-5872
                             Program Director: Dr. Thomas J. Lawley

Illinois   University of Illinois Hospital
                             1740 West Taylor Street
                             Chicago, IL 60612
                             (312) 996-3000
                             Program Director: Dr. Lawrence Solomon

Massachusetts	Massachusetts General Hospital 32 Fruit Street Boston, MA 02114 (617) 726-2000 Program Director: Dr. Howard P. Baden
Michigan	University of Michigan Hospitals 1500 East Medical Center Ann Arbor, MI 48109 (313) 936-4000 Program Director: Dr. Charles N. Ellis
Minnesota	Mayo Clinic 200 S. W. First Street Rochester, MN 55905 (507) 284-2511 Program Director: Dr. Sigfrid A. Muller
New Hampshire	Dartmouth-Hitchcock Medical Center 2 Maynard Street Hanover, NH 03756 (603) 646-5000 Program Director: Dr. Steven K. Spencer
New York	New York Hospital—Cornell Medical Center 525 East 68th Street New York, NY 10021 (212) 746-5454 Program Director: Dr. George W. Hambrick, Jr. Columbia-Presbyterian Medical Center 622 West 168th Street New York, NY 10032 (212) 305-2500 Program Director: Dr. Leonard C. Harber
North Carolina	Duke University Medical Center Box 3135 Durham, NC 27710 (919) 684-5587 Program Director: Dr. Sheldon R. Pinnell
Ohio	Cleveland Clinic Foundation 9500 Euclid Avenue Cleveland, OH 44106 (216) 444-2200 Program Director: Dr. Philip L. Ballin

Oklahoma   University of Oklahoma Health Sciences Center
                    619 N. E. 13th Street
                    Oklahoma City, OK 73104
                    (405) 271-4000
                    Program Director: Dr. Mark Everett

Pennsylvania   Hospital of the University of Pennsylvania
                    3400 Spruce Street
                    Philadelphia, PA 19104
                    (215) 662-6536
                    Program Director: Dr. Gerald S. Lazarus

Texas   University of Texas Southwestern Medical Center
                    5323 Harry Hines Boulevard
                    Dallas, TX 75235
                    (214) 688-2969
                    Program Director: Dr. Paul Bergstresser

                    Baylor College of Medicine and Hospitals
                    One Baylor Plaza
                    Houston, TX 77030
                    (713) 798-4951
                    Program Director: Dr. John Wolf, Jr.

Virginia   Medical College of Virginia Hospital
                    401 North 12th Street
                    Richmond, VA 23219
                    (804) 786-0932
                    Program Director: Dr. W. Kenneth Blaylock

ENDOCRINOLOGY

Endocrinology, a branch of internal medicine, studies the structure and functions of the glands that regulate the efficient performance of the body in a number of ways: temperature control, fluid intake and output, growth and development, rates of exchange of certain elements between various systems and the bloodstream, regulation of blood pressure, and control of the male and female reproductive organs, to name a few. The glands involved are regulated mainly by a master gland called the pituitary, which is located at the base of the brain. This gland, no larger than a pea, controls more than a dozen hormones which in turn stimulate (or retard) the hormone production of the other endocrine glands, such as the thyroid, parathyroid, pancreas, adrenals, ovaries, testes, thymus, and pineal. Knowledge of how hormonal mechanisms work is far from complete. Deficiencies in hormone production give rise to certain disease states that are usually well recognized clinically: goiter, softening and fracturing of bones, several kinds of diabetes, dwarfism, gigantism, and Addison's disease. In some

diseases the deficient hormones can be supplied over long or short periods of
time to restore normal function, and in certain cases where hormones have been
known to stimulate tumor growth, such growth may be impeded by the removal
of glands.

Alabama	University of Alabama Medical Center 619 South 19th Street/University Station Birmingham, AL 35294 (205) 934-3410 Program Director: Dr. Jeffrey Kudlow (Special interests: chemistry of diabetes and diabetic neuropathies)
Arizona	University of Arizona Health Sciences Center 1501 North Campbell Avenue Tucson, AZ 85724 (602) 626-0111 Program Director: Dr. David G. Johnson
California	University of California San Francisco Hospitals and Clinics 505 Parnassus Avenue San Francisco, CA 94143 (415) 476-1000 Program Director: Dr. Claude Arnaud
Florida	Shands Hospital—University of Florida 1600 S. W. Archer Road Gainesville, FL 32610 (904) 392-2612 Program Director: Dr. Thomas J. Merimee
Illinois	Rush-Presbyterian-St. Luke's Medical Center 1653 West Congress Parkway Chicago, IL 60612 (312) 942-7459 Program Director: Dr. John Bagdade Northwestern University Medical Center 250 East Superior Street Chicago, IL 60611 (312) 908-8022 Program Director: Dr. Norbert Freinkel
Maryland	Johns Hopkins Hospital 600 North Wolfe Street Baltimore, MD 21205 (301) 955-5000 Program Director: Dr. Simeon Margolis

Massachusetts	Lahey Clinic Foundation and Joslin Diabetes Center 41 Mall Road Burlington, MA 01805 (617) 273-8490 Program Director: Dr. Andre T. Guay
	Massachusetts General Hospital 32 Fruit Street Boston, MA 02114 (617) 726-2000 Program Director: Dr. Henry M. Kronenberg
Michigan	University of Michigan Hospitals 1500 East Medical Center Drive Ann Arbor, MI 48109 (313) 936-4000 Program Director: Dr. John C. Marshall
Minnesota	Mayo Clinic 200 S. W. First Street Rochester, MN 55905 (507) 284-2511 Program Director: Dr. Colum A. Gorman
Missouri	Barnes Hospital One Barnes Plaza St. Louis, MO 63110 (314) 362-5000 Program Director: Dr. Philip E. Cryer
New Mexico	University of New Mexico Hospital 2211 Lomas Boulevard, N. E. Albuquerque, NM 87106 (505) 843-2111 Program Director: Dr. R. Philip Eaton
North Carolina	University of North Carolina School of Medicine Chapel Hill, NC 27514 (919) 966-4161 Program Director: Dr. Timothy Gray
Ohio	Cleveland Clinic Foundation 9500 Euclid Avenue Cleveland, OH 44106 (216) 444-2200 Program Director: Dr. Leslie R. Sheeler

Pennsylvania	Hospital of the University of Pennsylvania 3400 Spruce Street Philadelphia, PA 19104 (215) 662-2300 Program Director: Dr. John G. Haddad, Jr.
Tennessee	Vanderbilt University Medical Center 1211 22nd Avenue, South Nashville, TN 37232 (615) 322-7311 Program Director: Dr. David N. Orth
Texas	Baylor College of Medicine and Hospitals One Baylor Plaza Houston, TX 77030 (713) 798-4951 Program Director: Dr. Aubrey E. Boyd
Utah	University of Utah Medical Center 50 North Medical Drive Salt Lake City, Utah 84132 (801) 581-2730 Program Director: Dr. Linscott M. Scott

GASTROENTEROLOGY

Gastroenterology is concerned with diseases of the digestive system. Digestion involves the intake of food, its conversion by chemical reactions into nutritional complexes for absorption in the intestine, and the elimination of waste products. Assisted by enzymes, hormones, and bacteria, different phases of digestion take place at different levels—from the saliva in the mouth to the billions of bacteria in the colon-rectal area breaking down waste products—under the regulatory mechanisms of the central nervous system.

Digestive diseases are usually classified on a regional basis: esophagus; stomach and the upper one-third of the small intestine; pancreas, liver, and gallbladder; the lower two-thirds of the small intestine; and the colon-rectal area. There is a long list of disorders affecting the digestive system, and the root causes of most of them are imperfectly understood. But their symptoms are usually quite apparent to the patient and the physician: appetite changes, nausea, vomiting, distention, pain that is regional or referred to other areas, constipation, diarrhea, bleeding, jaundice, and abnormal weight gain or loss.

A very researching history of the illness and a thorough clinical examination, plus a few well-selected tests will usually result in a correct diagnosis in most diseases of this system. Endoscopic examinations, special X-ray studies, chemical examinations, and bacteriologic studies—depending upon the particular symptoms of disease—usually confirm the type and extent of the disease.

Psychological factors also play an important part in understanding hunger, appetite failure, and the courses of certain diseases affecting the digestive tract.

Surgery is of course necessary for tumors, obstructions, perforations, certain vascular problems, most gallstones, and for some acute bacterial infections such as appendicitis. Most other conditions are treated by medicines. A number of surgical operations, devised for the treatment of nonthreatening conditions (particularly ulcers) seem logical from a mechanical standpoint, but such surgery is often unsuccessful because of a lack of understanding of the altered physiology that accompanies most of these operations. They may be resorted to, however, when there is a complete failure of response through medicinal means.

For this specialty, therefore, it is appropriate to combine the doctor-recommended lists for gastrointestinal medicine and gastrointestinal surgery, showing those institutions with strong departments in both.

California

University of California San Francisco Hospitals and Clinics
505 Parnassus Avenue
San Francisco, CA 94143
(415) 476-1000
Program Director (medicine): Dr. Robert K. Ockner
Program Director (surgery): Dr. Haile Debas
(Special interests: biliary tract, pancreas, stomach)

University of California San Diego Medical Center
225 West Dickinson Street
San Diego, CA 92103
(619) 294-6222
Program Director (medicine): Dr. Jon Isenberg
Program Director (surgery): Dr. Rahimor Moossa
(Special interests: pancreas, portal hypertension)

Florida

Shands Hospital—University of Florida
1600 S. W. Archer Road
Gainesville, FL 32610
(904) 392-2877
Program Director (medicine): Dr. Philip P. Toskes
Program Director (surgery): Dr. Edward Woodward
(Special interests: pancreas, stomach, gallbladder)

Illinois

University of Chicago Hospitals and Clinics
5841 South Maryland Avenue
Chicago, IL 60637
(312) 947-1000
Program Director (medicine): Dr. Nicholas O. Davidson
Program Director (surgery): Dr. George Black
(Special interests: inflammatory bowel diseases)

Maryland

Johns Hopkins Hospital
600 North Wolfe Street
Baltimore, MD 21205
(301) 955-5000
Program Director (medicine): Dr. Thomas Hendrix
Program Director (surgery): Dr. John Cameron
(Special interests: liver, bile ducts, pancreas)

Massachusetts

Beth Israel Hospital
330 Brookline Avenue
Boston, MA 02215
(617) 735-2000
Program Director (medicine): Dr. Raj Goyal
Program Director (surgery): Dr. William Silen
(Special interests: ulcers, liver, pancreas)

Lahey Clinic Foundation
41 Mall Road
Burlington, MA 01805
(617) 273-8740
Program Director (medicine): Dr. S. Peter Gibb
Program Director (surgery): Dr. Ricardo L. Rossi
(Special interests: bile ducts, pancreas)

Minnesota

University of Minnesota Hospitals
Harvard Street at East River Road
Minneapolis, MN 55455
(612) 626-3000
Program Director (medicine): Dr. Michael J. Shaw
Program Director (surgery): Dr. John Najarian
(Special interest: transplant surgery)

Mayo Clinic
200 S. W. First Street
Rochester, MN 55905
(507) 284-2511
Program Director (medicine): Dr. Albert D. New-
comer
Program Director (surgery): Dr. Clive S. Grant
(Special interest: bile duct surgery)

Missouri

University of Missouri Health Sciences Center
One Hospital Drive
Columbia, MO 65212
(314) 882-4141
Program Director (medicine): Dr. J. H. Butt
Program Director (surgery): Dr. Howard Reber
(Special interest: pediatric gastroenterology)

Barnes Hospital
One Barnes Plaza
St. Louis, MO 63110
(314) 362-5000
Program Director (medicine): Dr. David H. Alpers
Program Director (surgery): Dr. Samuel Well, Jr.

New York   Memorial Sloan-Kettering Cancer Center
1275 York Avenue
New York, NY 10021
(212) 794-6707
Program Director (medicine): Dr. Sidney Winawer
Program Director (surgery): Dr. Jerome DeCosse
(Special interest: cancer of the gastrointestinal tract)

Genesee Hospital
224 Alexander Street
Rochester, NY 14607
(716) 263-6160
Program Director (medicine): Dr. William Chey
Program Director (surgery): Dr. William Craver
(Special interests: inflammatory bowel diseases, sto-
    mach)

Ohio   Cleveland Clinic Foundation
9500 Euclid Avenue
Cleveland, OH 44106
(216) 444-2200
Program Director (medicine): Dr. William D. Carey
Program Director (surgery): Dr. Robert Hermann
(Special interests: pancreas, liver)

Pennsylvania Hospital of the University of Pennsylvania
3400 Spruce Street
Philadelphia, PA 19104
(215) 662-2168
Program Director (medicine): Dr. Frank P. Brooks
Program Director (surgery): Dr. Ernest Rosato
(Special interest: cancer of the gastrointestinal tract)

Presbyterian-University Hospital
De Sota and O'Hara Streets
Pittsburgh, PA 15213
(412) 648-9814
Program Director (medicine): Dr. David Van Thiel
Program Director (surgery): Dr. Thomas Starzl
(Special interest: leading U.S. center for liver trans-
    plant surgery)

Tennessee

Vanderbilt University Medical Center
1161 21st Avenue, South
Nashville, TN 37232
(615) 322-7311
Program Director (medicine): Dr. G. Dewey Dunn
Program Director (surgery): Dr. John Sawyers
(Special interests: stomach diseases)

Texas

University of Texas Southwestern Medical Center
5323 Harry Hines Boulevard
Dallas, TX 75235
(214) 688-3111
Program Director (medicine): Dr. Donald Seldin
Program Director (surgery): Dr. W. J. Fry

M. D. Anderson Hospital and Tumor Institute
6723 Bertner Drive
Houston, TX 77030
(713) 792-6170
Program Director (medicine): Dr. Martin Raber
Program Director (surgery): Dr. Frank Moody
(Special interest: gastrointestinal tract)

Virginia

Medical College of Virginia Hospital
401 North 12th Street
Richmond, VA 23219
(804) 786-0932
Program Director (medicine): Dr. Z. Reno Vlahcevic
Program Director (surgery): Dr. Walter Lawrence, Jr.
(Special interest: cancer of the gastrointestinal tract)

Washington

University of Washington Medical Center
1959 N. E. Pacific Street
Seattle, WA 98195
(206) 543-3183
Program Director (medicine): Dr. David R. Saunders
Program Director (surgery): Dr. Kaj Johansen

HEMATOLOGY

Hematology is the study of the blood, which may be considered an organ of the body with definite functions. Among these functions are the transportation of oxygen to the tissue (via hemoglobin), the transportation of nutritional elements to all areas of the body, and the removal of waste products. The blood also contains factors that defend against infection and provide immunity against allergy-producing matter.

The blood is a very sensitive indicator of diseases everywhere in the body. The recognition of changes in the composition of its cellular components and in the chemistry of its fluid elements greatly assists in the diagnosis of many diseases both apart from and including those of the blood itself. Red cells, white cells (of several types), and platelets (factors of blood coagulation and clotting) are the main cellular elements of the blood. Exactly how they are produced is not known, but normally there is an equilibrium between their rates of formation and destruction (when they wear out) so that their numbers individually and in proportion to each other are normally constant. The quality of these cellular elements is, of course, equally important. A skilled hematologist can accurately estimate their quantity and quality by the microscopic examination of a smear. Computerized blood counts are more accurate and time-saving than the old method of mechanical counting.

Abnormalities of the blood have numerous causes: lack of iron, cobalt, and other elements necessary for blood production; hormonal and vitamin deficiencies; genetic factors; liver and spleen disorders; the adverse effects of certain medicines; chemical and bacterial toxins; and parasitic infestations. Classification of blood diseases would require a number of pages of fine print, but the effects upon the blood of most of the diseases involve (1) increased or decreased production of a cellular element, (2) increased or decreased destruction of a cellular element, (3) changes in the normal relationship of cellular elements to the serum in which they are suspended, (4) changes in the quality and chemistry of any of the blood elements, and (5) bone-marrow changes that affect the formation of blood corpuscles.

In cases where a change in the blood picture is a reflection of diseases affecting other organs, a positive response to the treatment of the disease usually causes the blood to revert to its normal state. On the other hand, where a disease involves the blood-forming organs—of which the bone marrow is the most important—response to treatment usually depends upon whether the condition is benign or malignant. If owing to iron or vitamin deficiency, for example, improvement occurs; if owing to leukemia, response to treatment depends upon the type of leukemia present. Tremendous advances have been made in the treatment of some previously fatal leukemias in children through radiation and chemotherapy, with very long remissions in the majority of cases and apparent cures in quite a number. Chronic leukemia, chiefly affecting the middle-aged and older population, unfortunately, has a much less favorable outlook for treatment at the present time.

Another important interest of the hematologist is the collection, storing, typing, and dispensing of blood and blood elements for transfusion. Improved techniques in these fields have been one of the chief reasons for the advances in many types of surgery such as open-heart surgery and the transplantation of organs, both of which involve the replacement of considerable quantities of blood.

Alabama	University of Alabama Medical Center 619 South 19th Street/University Station Birmingham, AL 35294 (205) 934-5077 Program Director: Dr. Albert F. LoBuglio (Special interest: anemia)
California	Scripps Clinic and Research Foundation 10666 North Torey Pines Road La Jolla, CA 92037 (619) 455-9100 Program Director: Dr. Robert McMillan University of California San Francisco Hospitals and Clinics 505 Parnassus Avenue San Francisco, CA 94143 (415) 476-1000 Program Director: Dr. Marc Shuman
Connecticut	Yale–New Haven Hospital 333 Cedar Street New Haven, CT 06510 (203) 785-4242 Program Director: Dr. Edward J. Benz, Jr.
District of Columbia	George Washington University Hospital 901 23rd Street, N. W. Washington, DC 20037 (202) 994-1000 Program Director: Dr. Laurence S. Lessin
Florida	University of South Florida Medical Center 12901 North 30th Street Tampa, FL 33612 (813) 974-2201 Program Director: Dr. Hussain I. Saba University of Miami Affiliated Hospitals 1475 N. W. 12th Avenue Miami, FL 33136 (305) 547-6826 Program Director: Dr. William Harrington

Illinois

University of Illinois Hospital
1740 West Taylor Street
Chicago, IL 60612
(312) 996-3000
Program Director: Dr. Stanley G. Schade
(Special interest: anemia)

Maryland

Johns Hopkins Hospital
600 North Wolfe Street
Baltimore, MD 21205
(301) 955-5000
Program Director: Dr. Jerry L. Spivak
(Special interests: hemoglobin disorders)

Massachusetts

Brigham and Women's Hospital
75 Francis Street
Boston, MA 02115
(617) 732-5500
Program Director: Dr. Robert Handin

Tufts–New England Medical Center
171 Harrison Avenue
Boston, MA 02111
(617) 956-5000
Program Director: Dr. Robert S. Schwartz

Sidney Farber Cancer Institute
44 Binney Street
Boston, MA 02115
(617) 732-3000
Program Director: Dr. Emil Frei
(Special interests: lymphomas and leukemia in children)

Minnesota

University of Minnesota Hospitals
Harvard Street at East River Road
Minneapolis, MN 55455
(612) 626-3000
Program Director: Dr. Harry S. Jacob
(Outstanding in all phases of hematology)

Missouri

University of Missouri Health Sciences Center
One Hospital Drive
Columbia, MO 65212
(314) 882-4141
Program Director: Dr. John W. Yarbro

New York   St. Luke's Hospital
                      Amsterdam Avenue and 114th Street
                      New York, NY 10025
                      (212) 870-6000
                      Program Director: Dr. John F. Bertles

                      University Hospital—Upstate Medical Center
                      750 East Adams Street
                      Syracuse, NY 13210
                      (315) 473-5540
                      Program Director: Dr. Arlan Gottlieb

North Carolina   University of North Carolina School of Medicine
                      Chapel Hill, NC 27514
                      (919) 966-4161
                      Program Director: Dr. Harold Roberts
                      (Special interests: bleeding and clotting disorders)

                      Duke University Medical Center
                      Box 3005
                      Durham, NC 27710
                      (919) 684-5587
                      Program Director: Dr. Wendell Rosse

Pennsylvania   Hospital of the University of Pennsylvania
                      3400 Spruce Street
                      Philadelphia, PA 19104
                      (215) 662-3910
                      Program Director: Dr. Sanford J. Shattil
                      (Special interests: anemia, polycythemia)

Texas   University of Texas Center Southwestern Medical
                         Center
                      5323 Harry Hines Boulevard
                      Dallas, TX 75235
                      (214) 688-3111
                      Program Director: Dr. Eugene Frenkel

Utah   University of Utah Medical Center
                      50 North Medical Drive
                      Salt Lake City, Utah 84132
                      (801) 581-8158
                      Program Director: Dr. James P. Kushner

INTERNAL MEDICINE

The internist is essentially a diagnostician with a great deal more training than the general practitioner. He or she usually possesses considerably more experience in the selection of kinds of treatment and in measuring the effects of treatment—

particularly when dealing with medicines taken internally. He or she is concerned mainly with the disorders of the great organs systems of the body (heart and vascular system, lungs, gastrointestinal system, kidneys, and the lymphatic and blood-forming organs) and, to a somewhat lesser extent, with organs of special function such as the eye and ear.

Diseases of the great organs systems are often classified according to their causes: infectious diseases (bacterial, viral, parasitic, and so on); metabolic; neoplastic (tumors and diseases of the blood-forming organs); diseases of the immune regulatory systems; congenital diseases and deficiencies; and nutritional and environmental diseases. It can readily be seen that there is considerable overlap among these categories. For example, malaria may be classed as both a parasitic and an environmental disease, and some anemias are considered both congenital and nutritional. There are, of course, other ways of classifying diseases, such as by the organ systems involved and by the age of life when the disease primarily occurs.

Many internists, while remaining in command of the whole field of internal medicine, develop special interests in one or more of its subspecialties—hematology, endocrinology, kidney diseases, allergic conditions, rheumatics, gastrointestinal disorders, cardiorespiratory diseases, vascular diseases, and so on.

Even with the many diagnostic tools at hand, the internist today relies heavily upon a very complete medical history of the patient and a very thorough clinical examination. From these the internist is usually able to get a good idea of the kind and extent of the disease. He or she then knows what special tests are apt to help and which ones would be of little value. In many surgical cases the service of a skilled internist is necessary for the smooth management of pre- and postoperative treatment, especially when the patient has a number of health problems not all of which are the primary concern of the particular surgeon.

Although physicians who practice the specialty of internal medicine, strictly speaking, are not general or family practitioners, there is a great deal of confusion on this subject. Because of a shortage of general practice physicians in some areas of the country and the heavy trend toward specialization, thousands of people depend upon an internist as their primary physician.

| *Alabama* | University of Alabama Medical Center
619 South 19th Street/University Station
Birmingham, AL 35294
(205) 934-5304
Program Director: Dr. J. Claude Bennett |
| *California* | University of California San Francisco Hospitals and Clinics
505 Parnassus Avenue
San Francisco, CA 94143
(415) 476-1000
Program Director: Dr. Richard K. Root |

Stanford University Medical Center
300 Pasteur Drive
Stanford, CA 94305
(415) 723-4000
Program Director: Dr. Edward D. Harris, Jr.
(Especially noted for treatment of cardiovascular disease)

Colorado   University of Colorado Health Sciences Center
4200 East Ninth Avenue
Denver, CO 80262
(303) 329-3066
Program Director: Dr. Robert W. Schrier

Connecticut   Yale–New Haven Hospital
333 Cedar Street
New Haven, CT 06510
(203) 785-4242
Program Director: Dr. Robert M. Donaldson

District of   George Washington University Hospital
Columbia   901 23rd Street, N. W.
Washington, DC 20037
(202) 994-1000
Program Director: Dr. Gary Simon

Georgia   Emory University Hospital
1364 Clifton Road, N. E.
Atlanta, GA 30322
(404) 727-7050
Program Director: Dr. Juha P. Kokko

Illinois   Rush-Presbyterian-St. Luke's Medical Center
1653 West Congress Parkway
Chicago, IL 60612
(312) 942-5629
Program Director: Dr. Roger C. Bone

Indiana   Indiana University Medical Center
926 West Michigan Street
Indianapolis, IN 46223
(317) 635-8431
Program Director: Dr. August Watanabe

Kansas   University of Kansas Medical Center
39th Street and Rainbow Boulevard
Kansas City, KS 66103
(913) 588-5000
Program Director: Dr. Norton Greenberger

Kentucky	University of Kentucky Medical Center 800 Rose Street Lexington, KY 40563 (606) 233-5000 Program Director: Dr. John Thompson
	University of Louisville Hospital 530 South Jackson Street Louisville, KY 40202 (502) 562-3000 Program Director: Dr. Alfred Thompson, Jr.
Maryland	Johns Hopkins Hospital 600 North Wolfe Street Baltimore, MD 21205 (301) 955-5000 Program Director: Dr. John D. Stobo
Massachusetts	Massachusetts General Hospital 32 Fruit Street Boston, MA 02114 (617) 726-2000 Program Director: Dr. Andrew G. Bodnar
	Lahey Clinic Foundation 41 Mall Road Burlington, MA 01805 (617) 273-5100 Program Director: Dr. Eugene P. Clerkin (Noted for diabetes clinic and endocrinology research and treatment)
Michigan	University of Michigan Hospitals 1500 Medical Center Drive Ann Arbor, MI 48109 (313) 936-4000 Program Director: Dr. William Kelley
Minnesota	University of Minnesota Hospitals Harvard Street at East River Road Minneapolis, MN 55455 (612) 626-3000 Program Director: Dr. Thomas Ferris
	Mayo Clinic 200 S. W. First Street Rochester, MN 55905 (507) 284-2511 Program Director: Dr. Robert L. Frye

Missouri	Barnes Hospital One Barnes Plaza St. Louis, MO 63110 (314) 362-5000 Program Director: Dr. David Kipnis
New Hampshire	Dartmouth-Hitchcock Medical Center 2 Maynard Street Hanover, NH 03756 (603) 646-5000 Program Director: Dr. Jonathan Ross
New York	Mt. Sinai Hospital One Gustav Levy Place New York, NY 10029 (212) 650-6500 Program Director: Dr. Richard Gorlin
	New York University Medical Center 550 First Avenue New York, NY 10016 (212) 340-5505 Program Director: Dr. Saul Farber
	Columbia-Presbyterian Medical Center 622 West 168th Street New York, NY 10032 (212) 305-2500 Program Director: Dr. Robert Glickman
	City Hospital Center at Elmhurst 79–01 Broadway Elmhurst, NY 11373 (718) 830-1515 Program Director: Dr. Frank A. Ross (Especially noted for liver and pancreas treatment)
North Carolina	Duke University Medical Center Box 3703 Durham, NC 27710 (919) 684-5587 Program Director: Dr. Joseph C. Greenfield, Jr.
	Bowman Gray School of Medicine of Wake Forest University North Carolina Baptist Hospital 300 South Hawthorne Road Winston-Salem, NC 27103 (919) 748-2020 Program Director: Dr. William R. Hazzard

Ohio	Cleveland Clinic Foundation 9500 Euclid Avenue Cleveland, OH 44106 (216) 444-2200 Program Director: Dr. Steven A. Ockner (Noted for treatment of hypertension and cardiovascular and kidney diseases)
Pennsylvania	Hospital of the University of Pennsylvania 3400 Spruce Street Philadelphia, PA 19104 (215) 662-2402 Program Director: Dr. Laurence E. Earley
	Hahnemann University Hospital Broad and Vine Streets Philadelphia, PA 19102 (215) 448-7000 Program Director: Dr. Allan B. Schwartz
	Presbyterian-University Hospital De Sota and O'Hara Streets Pittsburgh, PA 15213 (412) 648-9641 Program Director: Dr. Gerald S. Levey
	Shadyside Hospital 5230 Centre Avenue Pittsburgh, PA 15232 (412) 622-2121 Program Director: Dr. Alvin B. Shapiro (Also known for cardiology and cardiac surgery)
Tennessee	Baptist Memorial Hospital 899 Madison Avenue Memphis, TN 38146 (901) 522-5252 Program Director: Dr. James B. Lewis, Jr.
	Baptist Hospital 2000 Church Street Nashville, TN 37236 (615) 329-5555 Program Director: Dr. Paul McNabb

Texas	University of Texas Southwestern Medical Center
	5323 Harry Hines Boulevard
	Dallas, TX 75235
	(214) 688-3486
	Program Director: Dr. Daniel Foster
Virginia	University of Virginia Hospital
	Jefferson Park Avenue
	Charlottesville, VA 22908
	(804) 924-0211
	Program Director: Dr. Edward Hook
Washington	University of Washington Medical Center
	1959 N. E. Pacific Street
	Seattle, WA 98195
	(206) 543-1060
	Program Director: Dr. Philip J. Fialkon
Wisconsin	University of Wisconsin Hospital and Clinics
	600 Highland Avenue
	Madison, WI 53792
	(608) 263-1771
	Program Director: Dr. Richard B. Friedman
	Mt. Sinai Medical Center
	950 North 12th Street
	Milwaukee, WI 53201
	(414) 289-8200
	Program Director: Dr. Richard Rielselbach

NEPHROLOGY

Among the principal organs for the elimination of wastes from the body, the kidneys function as a filtration system that selectively reabsorbs and recycles useful elements before eliminating only a small portion of the total amount filtered as urine.

Efficient function depends upon the various parts of the kidneys working together. Particularly important are the capillaries and blood vessels. High blood pressure in a patient may be caused by the narrowing of the renal vessels. Under certain conditions, the kidneys may produce a chemical that raises the blood pressure affecting the size of arteries elsewhere in the body, as well as those of the kidneys themselves. Diabetes and bone diseases may also affect the kidneys, and inflammatory diseases of the kidneys may affect other organs. A number of chemicals and medicinal substances are toxic to the kidneys, and allergic reactions and shock may depress kidney function temporarily or permanently.

In the past, the outlook was bleak for patients suffering from irreversible kidney failure. Now such patients are kept alive by several methods of dialysis—the removal of waste products that is performed either outside the body or within the abdominal cavity. Kidney transplants are preferable to and cheaper than dialysis, but the number of patients in need of such operations is much greater than the supply of suitable donor kidneys. The kidney was the first organ to be transplanted and is still the most frequently performed transplant. The results of such operations are the best of all organ transplants.

Kidney stones are discussed in more detail in the section on urology (see page 105). Diets of several types and various medicines apparently help prevent the formation of some types of stones, but once they have formed they are usually treated surgically. New methods of kidney stone removal are designed to fragment them and remove the pieces through minimally invasive operations.

Nephrology is an important part of internal medicine, and most problems affecting the kidneys are managed well by the internist. Some internists, however, have become specialists in this field. The following list indicates those centers with outstanding nephrology departments.

Alabama   University of Alabama Medical Center
                     619 South 19th Street/University Station
                     Birmingham, AL 35294
                     (205) 934-3585
                     Program Director: Dr. David G. Warnock

Arkansas   University of Arkansas for Medical Sciences
                     4301 West Markham Street
                     Little Rock, AR 72205
                     (501) 661-5000
                     Program Director: Dr. John E. Buerkert

California   University of California Los Angeles School of Medi-
                        cine
                     10833 Le Conte Avenue
                     Los Angeles, CA 90024
                     (213) 825-4321
                     Program Director: Dr. Leon G. Fine

                     University of California San Francisco Hospitals and
                        Clinics
                     505 Parnassus Avenue
                     San Francisco, CA 94143
                     (415) 476-1000
                     Program Director: Dr. Floyd C. Rector

Colorado	University of Colorado Health Sciences Center 4200 East Ninth Avenue Denver, CO 80262 (303) 329-3066 Program Director: Dr. Robert Schrier
Connecticut	Yale–New Haven Hospital 333 Cedar Street New Haven, CT 06510 (203) 785-4242 Program Director: Dr. John Hayslett
District of Columbia	Georgetown University Hospital 3800 Reservoir Road, N. W. Washington, DC 20007 (202) 625-7001 Program Director: Dr. William P. Argy
Illinois	University of Illinois Hospital 1740 West Taylor Street Chicago, IL 60612 (312) 996-3000 Program Director: Dr. Jose A. L. Arruda
Massachusetts	Massachusetts General Hospital 32 Fruit Street Boston, MA 02114 (617) 726-2000 Program Director: Dr. Cecil Coggins
	Brigham and Women's Hospital 75 Francis Street Boston, MA 02115 (617) 732-5500 Program Director: Dr. Barry Brenner
Minnesota	University of Minnesota Hospitals Harvard Street at East River Road Minneapolis, MN 55455 (612) 626-3000 Program Director: Dr. Thomas H. Hostetter
Missouri	University of Missouri Health Sciences Center One Hospital Drive Columbia, MO 65212 (314) 882-4141 Program Director: Dr. Karl Nolph

Barnes Hospital
One Barnes Plaza
St. Louis, MO 63110
(314) 362-5000
Program Director: Dr. Saul Klahr

New York
New York University Medical Center
550 First Avenue
New York, NY 10016
(212) 340-5505
Program Director: Dr. David Baldwin

Strong Memorial Hospital, University of Rochester
    Medical Center
601 Elmwood Avenue
Rochester, NY 14642
(716) 275-4517
Program Director: Dr. Daniel B. Ornt

Ohio
University of Cincinnati Hospital
234 Goodman Street
Cincinnati, OH 45267
(513) 558-1000
Program Director: Dr. Victor Pollak

Cleveland Clinic Foundation
9500 Euclid Avenue
Cleveland, OH 44106
(216) 444-2200
Program Director: Dr. Phillip Hall

Pennsylvania
Hospital of the University of Pennsylvania
3400 Spruce Street
Philadelphia, PA 19104
(215) 662-2638
Program Director: Dr. Zalman S. Agus

Tennessee
Vanderbilt University Medical Center
1211 22nd Avenue, South
Nashville, TN 37232
(615) 322-7311
Program Director: Dr. Richard L. Gibson

Texas
University of Texas Southwestern Medical Center
5323 Harry Hines Boulevard
Dallas, TX 75235
(214) 688-3486
Program Director: Dr. Daniel Foster

Washington   University of Washington Medical Center
                        1959 N. E. Pacific Street
                        Seattle, WA 98195
                        (206) 548-3300
                        Program Director: Dr. William G. Conser

Wisconsin   Medical College of Wisconsin
                        8700 West Wisconsin Avenue
                        Milwaukee, WI 53226
                        (414) 259-3070
                        Program Director: Dr. Jacob Lemann, Jr.

NEUROLOGY
(see also chapter 4, "Surgery")

Neurology deals with the diagnostic and nonsurgical treatment of disorders of the nervous system. The components of this system include the brain, the vast cablelike structures of the spinal cord (which carry messages to and from the brain), and the distant structures (muscles, tendons, blood vessels, joints, glands, and the various organ systems of the body) which receive and send messages through their nerve branches to the spinal cord and the brain. Much of the electrical traffic along these "wires" takes place automatically in such a way that the areas of the brain that govern consciousness are not aware that this activity is constantly going on. For example, one is not aware of the continuous adjustments governed by the nervous system in the size of the ocular pupil in response to the varying amounts of light that enter the eye. Other functions of the nervous system are under control of the conscious will: the desire to walk, swim, dance, or sing. Often, both automatic and conscious mechanisms are involved at nearly the same time: If one touches a hot stove, the act that withdraws the hand is reflexive and takes place in the spinal cord before the sensation of abnormal heat reaches the brain.

Although it has long been possible to make informed guesses as to the general location of disease or injury affecting certain nerve functions, physicians now can pinpoint accurately even small areas of nerve-tissue destruction or malfunction. Improved localization of disorders within the nervous system is possible mainly through improved X-ray techniques, which involve three-dimensional pictures (i.e., computerized scanning), arteriography and, most recently, magnetic resonance imaging (MRI). These improvements in diagnosis have been in the direction of noninvasive methods, eliminating many of the dangers of previous methods.

Neurology is also being advanced by other techniques such as the computerized analysis of responses to sound and light impulses, the chemistry of nerve impulses, measurements of the speed of conduction along nerve fibers, and the identification of specific cell receptors that regulate pain sensation. Unfortunately, progress has been much slower in discovering the causes of certain serious afflictions of nerve tissue, such as multiple sclerosis.

Alabama
University of Alabama Medical Center
619 South 19th Street/University Station
Birmingham, AL 35294
(205) 934-2402
Program Director: Dr. John N. Whitaker
(Special interest: pediatric neurology)

California
University of California San Francisco Hospitals and
Clinics
505 Parnassus Avenue
San Francisco, CA 94143
(415) 476-1000
Program Director: Dr. Robert Fishman

Colorado
University of Colorado Health Sciences Center
4200 East Ninth Avenue
Denver, CO 80262
(303) 329-3066
Program Director: Dr. Donald H. Gilden

District of
Columbia
Children's Hospital National Medical Center
111 Michigan Avenue, N. W.
Washington, DC 20010
(202) 745-5000
Program Director: Dr. G. F. Molinari
(Special interests: neurological diseases of children)

Maryland
Johns Hopkins Hospital
600 North Wolfe Street
Baltimore, MD 21205
(301) 955-5000
Program Director: Dr. Guy McKhann
(Special interests: neuromuscular diseases, peripheral
nerve disorders, viral diseases of the central nervous system, multiple sclerosis)

Massachusetts
Massachusetts General Hospital
32 Fruit Street
Boston, MA 02114
(617) 726-2000
Program Director: Dr. Joseph Martin

Children's Hospital '
300 Longwood Avenue
Boston, MA 02115
(617) 735-6000
Program Director: Dr. Charles Barlow

Minnesota

Mayo Clinic
200 S. W. First Street
Rochester, MN 55905
(507) 284-2511
Program Director: Dr. B. A. Sandok
(Special interests: peripheral nerve disorders, neuromuscular diseases)

Missouri

Barnes Hospital
One Barnes Plaza
St. Louis, MO 63110
(314) 362-7177
Program Director: Dr. William Landau
(Special interests: neuromuscular diseases)

New York

Neurological Institute, Columbia-Presbyterian Medical
Center
710 West 168th Street
New York, NY 10032
(212) 305-2500
Program Director: Dr. Lewis Rowland
(Special interests: neuromuscular diseases, strokes,
speech disorders)

New York Hospital—Cornell Medical Center
525 East 68th Street
New York, NY 10021
(212) 746-5454
Program Director: Dr. Fred Plum
(Special interests: Parkinson's disease, multiple sclerosis)

Strong Memorial Hospital, University of Rochester
Medical Center
601 Elmwood Avenue
Rochester, NY 14642
(716) 275-2541
Program Director: Dr. Robert C. Griggs
(Special interest: multiple sclerosis)

North Carolina	Bowman Gray School of Medicine of Wake Forest University North Carolina Baptist Hospital 300 South Hawthorne Road Winston-Salem, NC 27103 (919) 748-4643 Program Director: Dr. B. Todd Troost (Special interests: cerebrovascular disorders)
Ohio	Children's Hospital Medical Center Elland and Bethesda Avenues Cincinnati, OH 45229 (513) 559-4200 Program Director: Dr. Harold E. Booker (Special interest: pediatric neurology)
Pennsylvania	Hospital of the University of Pennsylvania 3400 Spruce Street Philadelphia, PA 19104 (215) 662-3386 Program Director: Dr. Donald H. Silberberg (Special interests: multiple sclerosis, neuromuscular diseases, pediatric neurology) Hahnemann University Hospital Broad and Vine Streets Philadelphia, PA 19102 (215) 448-7000 Program Director: Dr. Elliot Mancall Presbyterian-University Hospital De Sota and O'Hara Streets Pittsburgh, PA 15213 (412) 648-9641 Program Director: Dr. Oscar Reinmuth (Special interests: comprehensive epilepsy center, stroke prevention)
Texas	Baylor College of Medicine and Hospitals One Baylor Plaza Houston, TX 77030 (713) 798-4951 Program Director: Dr. R. M. Armstrong

Virginia   University of Virginia Hospital
                         Jefferson Park Avenue
                         Charlottesville, VA 22908
                         (804) 924-0211
                         Program Director: Dr. T. R. Johns
                         (Special interests: neuromuscular diseases, myasthenia
                             gravis, epilepsy)

Washington   University of Washington Medical Center
                         1959 N. W. Pacific Street
                         Seattle, WA 98195
                         (206) 543-2340
                         Program Director: Dr. Phillip Swanson
                         (Special interests: Parkinson's disease, epilepsy,
                             strokes)

PULMONARY MEDICINE

The chief functions of the lungs are to supply adequate amounts of oxygen to the circulating blood for delivery to all parts of the body and to remove excess amounts of waste gases, mainly carbon dioxide, from the body. This is accomplished by chemical reactions occuring in the blood capillaries of the millions of tiny air sacs located in the lungs. For these chemical reactions to take place, there must be a constant amount of air being moved in and out of the lungs through the process called ventilation. Anything that obstructs the normal flow of air to and from the lung capillaries interferes with the respiratory function.

Diseases affecting almost any part of the body may, with their many ramifications, involve the lungs at some stage. Of these, heart disease is the most striking because efficient lung function depends upon efficient heart action to supply constant amounts of blood to the lungs for aeration and to transport the aerated blood to the various parts of the body.

Of the many kinds of pulmonary disease, some examples are infections involving one or more parts of the bronchial tree caused by bacteria, fungi, parasites, or other agents, and complications arising from these infections; congenital abnormalities such as respiratory distress syndrome in the newborn; diseases of the blood vessels, including those located in the lungs; certain disorders of the immune mechanisms; emboli; tumors (benign and malignant); emphysema; and occupational diseases such as silicosis, anthracosis, and asbestosis.

Diagnosis of lung disease involves endoscopic visualization of the tracheobronchial tree, X rays of the chest, pulmonary function tests designed to measure efficiency, chemical analysis of the blood, and studies of heart function. Treatment of the vast majority of pulmonary conditions is medical rather than surgical. Foreign bodies and tumors, of course, require surgical removal.

Pulmonary medicine is an important subspecialty of internal medicine, and one may expect to find in the teaching institutions good facilities for the diagnosis and treatment of lung conditions, with one or more staff members having a special interest in this field.

Alabama	University of Alabama Medical Center 619 South 19th Street/University Station Birmingham, AL 35294 (205) 934-5411 Program Director: Dr. Richard Briggs, Jr.
Arkansas	University of Arkansas for Medical Sciences 4301 West Markham Street Little Rock, AR 72205 (501) 686-5000 Program Director: Dr. F. Charles Hiller
California	University of California Davis Medical Center 4301 X Street Sacramento, CA 95817 (916) 453-3096 Program Director: Dr. C. E. Cross
Colorado	University of Colorado Health Sciences Center 4200 East Ninth Avenue Denver, CO 80262 (303) 329-3066 Program Director: Dr. James H. Fisher
Connecticut	Winchester Chest Clinic Yale–New Haven Hospital 333 Cedar Street New Haven, CT 06510 (203) 785-4242 Program Director: Dr. Herbert Reynolds
Illinois	University of Chicago Hospitals and Clinics 5841 South Maryland Avenue Chicago, IL 60637 (312) 947-1000 Program Director: Dr. Lawrence Wood
Indiana	Indiana University Medical Center 926 West Michigan Street Indianapolis, IN 46223 (317) 635-8431 Program Director: Dr. Robert Stonehill

Maryland	Johns Hopkins Hospital 600 North Wolfe Street Baltimore, MD 21205 (301) 955-5000 Program Director: Dr. Wilmot Ball, Jr.
Massachusetts	Boston University School of Medicine 80 East Concord Street Boston, MA 02118 (617) 638-8000 Program Director: Dr. David M. Center
	Brigham and Women's Hospital 75 Francis Street Boston, MA 02115 (617) 732-5500 Program Director: Dr. Roland Ingram, Jr.
Michigan	University of Michigan Hospitals 1500 East Medical Center Drive Ann Arbor, MI 48109 (313) 936-4000 Program Director: Dr. Galen B. Toews
Minnesota	Mayo Clinic 200 S. W. First Street Rochester, MN 55905 (507) 284-2511 Program Director: Dr. E. C. Rosenow III
New York	New York University Medical Center, Bellevue Hospital Center First Avenue and 27th Street New York, NY 10016 (212) 340-5505 Program Director: Dr. H. William Harris
North Carolina	Duke University Medical Center Box 3703 Durham, NC 27710 (919) 684-5587 Program Director: Dr. James Crapo
Pennsylvania	Hospital of the University of Pennsylvania 3400 Spruce Street Philadelphia, PA 19104 (215) 662-3202 Program Director: Dr. Alfred P. Fishman

Presbyterian-University Hospital
De Sota and O'Hara Streets
Pittsburgh, PA 15213
(412) 648-9350
Program Director: Dr. Robert M. Rogers
(Special interests: bronchopulmonary lavage, sleep
    disorders)

Tennessee

Vanderbilt University Hospital
1211 22nd Avenue, South
Nashville, TN 37232
(615) 322-7311
Program Director: Dr. Kenneth L. Brigham

Texas

Baylor College of Medicine and Hospitals
One Baylor Plaza
Houston, TX 77030
(713) 798-4951
Program Director: Dr. R. Keith Wilson

University of Texas Southwestern Medical Center
5323 Harry Hines Boulevard
Dallas, TX 75235
(214) 688-3111
Program Director: Dr. Alan Pierce

Utah

University of Utah Medical Center
50 North Medical Drive
Salt Lake City, UT 84132
(801) 581-7806
Program Director: Dr. John R. Hoidal

Washington

University of Washington Medical Center
1959 N. E. Pacific Street
Seattle, WA 98195
(206) 543-3166
Program Director: Dr. Leonard Hudson

· 4 ·
SURGERY: THE AGE OF NEW DEVELOPMENTS

Gone are the days of the surgeon who was expected to be able to operate upon all parts of the body from head to toe. The wonder is not that he or she was able to do so little as compared with today's surgeon, but that he or she was able to accomplish so much with the limited resources available. That surgeon has left a valuable legacy of surgical principles as the firm foundation upon which all modern surgery rests.

Surgery nowadays is compartmentalized into systems and regions of the body, and even within particular areas, surgeons may narrow their field of interest to only a few operations. The skill and experience thus acquired account for increasing travel on the part of the patient to the localities of the "superspecialists." Teams of surgeons, working in teaching hospitals and with the experience of hundreds of various cases of a given disorder, have a great deal more to offer the patient with a difficult problem than a surgeon working alone in a community hospital, whose experience may be limited to a few cases of a particular type per year.

If a single favorable thing can be said about wars, with all their horrors, it is that they have had a dramatic impact upon the speed of medical and surgical advances. Penicillin, the most marvelous of all antimicrobial drugs, was developed during World War II and became generally available to civilian populations after 1945. Its use immediately broadened the horizons of surgery by sharply decreasing disability and mortality from wound infections. Newer generations of antibiotics, when properly used, also help to make more and more extensive surgery possible.

Another important advance in the field of surgery was the invention of a process for the drying and storage of blood plasma by the late Dr. Max Strumia, hematologist at the Bryn Mawr Hospital in Pennsylvania. This process saved countless lives on World War II battlefields—lives that otherwise would have been lost through shock resulting from hemorrhage.

It was soon recognized that, in addition to cutting and sewing well, other factors were equally important to successful surgery. The special requirements of the surgical patient for adequate fluids with balanced chemical and nutritional elements began to receive intensive study, with improved healing of wounds and rapid recovery from surgery the result. Recently developed methods of breaking down blood components have helped to make possible extensive operations requiring vast amounts of a particular element.

Of all the disciplines helpful to modern surgery, none is more important than the science of anesthesiology. Progess in this field, permitting extensive and sometimes long operations, has been mainly in the direction of better premedication and the search for anesthetic agents that are less toxic, nonexplosive, and muscle relaxing. Each stage of general anesthesia is monitored for safety and effectiveness, and in the medical-college hospitals, every anesthetic administration is a teaching exercise in physiology.

Diagnostic aids to surgery (in additional to conventional X-ray techniques and laboratory procedures) include some newer techniques that are either non- or minimally invasive. Among these techniques are fiberoptic endoscopy, computerized axial tomography (CAT) scan, ultrasound imaging, magnetic resonance imaging (MRI), and positron emission tomography (PET). Any of these in a particular situation may help the surgeon to plan the extent and limits of an operation before he or she begins. The development of the operating microscope, with its high degree of image resolution and magnification, has also benefited many of the surgical specialties; it has made possible fine stitching of severed nerves and blood vessels, which has helped to save limbs badly damaged or even severed after accidents or debilitated by intrinsic disease. Surgery of the ear and of the eye has been particularly advanced by the operating microscope.

BURN CARE

Victims of severe burn injury, the nation's third leading cause of accidental death, must be taken *immediately,* by plane or helicopter if necessary, to the nearest burn center. There, specially trained surgical teams are ready at all times to save lives that may have been lost previously because of delay, infection, and other medical complications. Badly burned accident victims require immediate treatment to prevent the loss of vital body fluids. Within the past several years, 185 burn centers have been developed throughout the United States in answer to a fast-growing need. We suggest that you make a mental note of the burn center nearest you in case such an emergency should arise.

The lifesaving work of the burn centers will soon be greatly enhanced by the availability of two exciting medical discoveries, both developed at the laboratories of Massachusetts General Hospital. First, a team of laboratory technicians under Dr. Howard Green has discovered how to stimulate the growth of the burn victim's own skin (it can cover an area from the size of a postage stamp to a square yard in a three-week period). The second discovery is the creation of man-made skin by Dr. John F. Burke with Ioannis V. Yannis, of the Massachusetts Institute of Technology. Approved by the Food and Drug Administration in 1984, this artificial skin has been successfully used on a number of burn patients. Other devices being employed in the treatment of severe burns are MRI, which can detect changes caused by the burn to the body's sugars, fats, and carbohydrates, and an ultrasound, high-frequency device that enables physicians to assess the precise depth of a burn soon after injury.

Some of the larger regional burn centers in the United States include:

California   University of Southern California Medical Center
                            Burn Unit
                        1200 North State Street
                        Los Angeles, CA 90033
                        (213) 226-2345
                        Program Director: Dr. Bruce Zawacki

Florida   Jackson Memorial Hospital
                            Burn Center
                        1611 N. W. 12th Avenue
                        Miami, FL 33136
                        (305) 325-7429
                        Program Directors: Dr. C. Gillon Ward
                        Dr. Jeffrey Hammond

Illinois   Sumner L. Koch Burn Center
                            Cook County Hospital
                        1835 West Harrison Street
                        Chicago, IL 60612
                        (312) 633-6000
                        Program Director: Dr. T. Mat Suda

Massachusetts   Shriner's Burn Institute
                        51 Blossom Street
                        Boston, MA 02114
                        (617) 722-3000
                        Program Director: Dr. Salvator Russo

New York   Cornell University Medical Center
                            Burn Division
                        525 East 68th Street
                        New York, NY 10021
                        (212) 746-5454
                        Program Director: Brian Feit

Ohio	Shriner's Burn Institute 202 Goodman Street Cincinnati, OH 45219 (513) 751-3900 Program Director: Ronald Hitzler
Tennessee	University Physicians Foundation (Affiliated with University of Tennessee) 951 Court Avenue Memphis, TN 38103 (901) 528-6610 Program Director: Dr. William L. Hickerson
Texas	Army Institute of Surgical Research Ft. Sam Houston San Antonio, TX 78234 (512) 221-2720
	Parkland Memorial Hospital 5201 Harry Hines Boulevard Dallas, TX 75235 (214) 590-8011 (Special interests of this regional burn center include skin graft techniques, infection control, and nutritional support for burn patients. Affiliated with University of Texas–Southwestern Medical Center)
Washington	Harborview Medical Center Burn Unit 325 Ninth Avenue Seattle, WA 98104 (206) 223-3000 Program Director: Dr. David Heimbach)

For the name of the nearest burn center in your region, we suggest that you call your local dermatologist. With the number of treatment centers still increasing, most major cities in the United States are now equipped to handle severely burned accident victims.

CARDIOTHORACIC SURGERY

Cardiothoracic surgery involves a team approach. For many types of operations, the heart must be stopped for varying periods during which a heart-lung machine—much modified since its invention by Dr. John Gibbon in 1953— performs the function of the heart, by circulating the blood, and of the lungs, by oxygenating the blood and removing impurities from it.

The most frequently performed heart operation is the coronary bypass, the object of which is to connect healthy portions of one or more arteries to bypass diseased areas. At first, vein material was more commonly used, but now it has been found that certain arteries located near the heart are better sources of grafts because they are similar in size, are otherwise more like the coronaries, and they usually hold up longer than vein grafts.

Other methods of overcoming coronary artery narrowing include balloon angioplasty, which stretches the arterial walls, and laser reduction of occluding tissue. Neither has been found to be entirely satisfactory over the long run. More promising at present is coronary atherectomy. In this procedure, a catheter, at the end of which is a tiny capsule containing a tiny rotatable blade, is threaded to the point of arterial obstruction and then cuts away diseased lining. A high degree of accuracy is made possible by computerized images immediately available to the surgical team as the operation progresses. The patient is awake and is able to communicate sensations. Postoperative discomfort is usually quite minimal, and hospitalization usually lasts no more than two days.

Improved medical methods of treating coronary disease must be taken into account. Before submitting to any type of heart surgery, patients are advised to seek a second or even third opinion as to the indications and necessity for it.

Alabama

University of Alabama Medical Center
619 South 19th Street/University Station
Birmingham, AL 35294
(205) 934-5200
Program Director: Dr. Arnold G. Diethelm

California

University of California San Francisco Hospitals and
    Clinics
505 Parnassus Avenue
San Francisco, CA 94143
(415) 476-1000
Program Director: Dr. Donald Magilligan

University of California Los Angeles Medical Center
10833 Le Conte Avenue
Los Angeles, CA 90024
(213) 825-4321
Program Director: Dr Hillel Laks
(Special interests: cardiac surgery for children)

Hospital of the Good Samaritan
1235 Wilshire Boulevard
Los Angeles, CA 90017
(213) 977-2121
Program Director: Dr. Richard Hughes

Stanford University Medical Center
300 Pasteur Drive
Stanford, CA 94305
(415) 723-4000
Program Director: Dr. Norman E. Shumway
(Special interests: heart and heart-lung transplants)

Florida

Jackson Memorial Hospital
1611 N. W. 12th Avenue
Miami, FL 33136
(305) 325-7429
Program Director: Dr. Gerard Kaiser

Georgia

Emory University Hospital
1364 Clifton Road, N. E.
Atlanta, GA 30322
(404) 727-7021
Program Director: Dr. Charles Hatcher

Illinois

Northwestern University Medical Center
250 East Superior Street
Chicago, IL 60611
(312) 908-2000
Program Director: Dr. Lawrence Michaelis

University of Chicago Hospitals and Clinics
5841 South Maryland Avenue
Chicago, IL 60637
(312) 947-1000
Program Director: Dr. Thomas J. Krizek

Louisiana

Alton Ochsner Medical Foundation
1516 Jefferson Highway
New Orleans, LA 70121
(504) 838-3000
Program Director: Dr. John Ochsner

Massachusetts

Massachusetts General Hospital
32 Fruit Street
Boston, MA 02114
(617) 726-2000
Program Director: Dr. Hermes C. Grillo

Brigham and Women's Hospital
75 Francis Street
Boston, MA 02115
(617) 732-5500
Program Director: Dr. Lawrence H. Cohn

Children's Hospital
300 Longwood Avenue
Boston, MA 02115
(617) 735-6000
Program Director: Dr. Lawrence H. Cohn
(Special interest: cardiac surgery for children)

Michigan

University of Michigan Medical Center
1500 Medical Center Drive
Ann Arbor, MI 48109
(313) 936-4000
Program Director: Dr. Mark B. Orringer

Minnesota

Mayo Clinic
200 S. W. First Street
Rochester, MN 55905
(507) 284-2511
Program Director: Dr. G. K. Danielson

Missouri

Barnes Hospital
One Barnes Plaza
St. Louis, MO 63110
(314) 362-7260
Program Director: Dr. James W. Cox

New York

New York University Medical Center
First Avenue and 27th Street
New York, NY 10016
(212) 340-5505
Program Director: Dr. Stephen B. Colvin

Columbia-Presbyterian Medical Center
622 West 168th Street
New York, NY 10032
(212) 305-2500
Program Director: Dr. James R. Malm
(Special interests: cardiac surgery for children)

North Carolina

Duke University Medical Center
Box 3005
Durham, NC 27710
(916) 684-5587
Program Director: Dr. David Sabiston, Jr.

Ohio	Cleveland Clinic Foundation 9500 Euclid Avenue Cleveland, OH 44106 (216) 444-2200 Program Director: Dr. Floyd Loop
	University of Cincinnati Hospital 234 Goodman Street Cincinnati, OH 45267 (513) 558-1000 Program Director: Dr. John Flege, Jr.
Pennsylvania	Hospital of the University of Pennsylvania 3400 Spruce Street Philadelphia, PA 19104 (215) 662-2050 Program Director: Dr. L. Henry Edmunds, Jr.
Tennessee	Vanderbilt University Medical Center 1211 22nd Street, South Nashville, TN 37232 (615) 322-7311 Program Director: Dr. Harvey Bender (Special interest: cardiac surgery for children)
Texas	Texas Heart Institute 6720 Bertner Drive Houston, TX 77030 (713) 791-4011 Program Director: Dr. Denton Cooley
	Baylor College of Medicine and Hospitals One Baylor Plaza Houston, TX 77030 (713) 798-4951 Program Director: Dr. Michael DeBakey
	Texas Children's Hospital 6621 Fannin Street Houston, TX 77030 (713) 798-1000 Program Director: Dr. Denton Cooley (Special interest: cardiac surgery for children)
Utah	University of Utah Medical Center 50 North Medical Drive Salt Lake City, UT 84132 (801) 581-7304 Program Director: Dr. William A. Gay, Jr.

Washington

University of Washington Medical Center
1959 N. E. Pacific Street
Seattle, WA 98195
(206) 543-3093
Program Director: Dr. Tom D. Ivey

COLON AND RECTAL SURGERY

Tumors, often malignant, account for a vast number of the colon and rectal surgical procedures performed today. As such, they also fall into the field of the surgical oncologist (cancer specialist), possibly requiring treatment in a specialized cancer care center. Of course, surgical procedures for nonmalignant conditions also require the best available talent. The trained surgical team, with experience working as a unit, the newest radiology equipment, and a skilled nursing staff greatly facilitate this type of surgery. The following medical centers, all with residency programs in this specialty, have special colon-rectal surgical teams.

California

Cottage Hospital
Pueblo at Bath Street
Santa Barbara, CA 93102
(805) 682-7111
Program Director: Dr. Elliot Prager

Illinois

Cook County Hospital
1835 West Harrison Street
Chicago, IL 60612
(312) 633-6000
Program Director: Dr. Herand Abcarian

Michael Reese Hospital
Lake Shore Drive at 31st Street
Chicago, IL 60616
(312) 791-2000
Program Director: Dr. Gerald Moss

Carle Foundation Hospital
611 West Park Street
Urbana, IL 61801
(217) 337-3311
Program Director: Dr. Howard D. Robertson

Louisiana

Louisiana State University Hospital
1541 Kings Highway
Shreveport, LA 71130
(318) 674-5000
Program Director: Dr. H. Whitney Boggs, Jr.

Alton Ochsner Medical Foundation
1516 Jefferson Highway
New Orleans, LA 70121
(504) 838-3000
Program Director: Dr. J. Byron Gaithright, Jr.

Massachusetts

Lahey Clinic Foundation
41 Mall Road
Burlington, MA 01805
(617) 273-8571
Program Director: Dr. David J. Schoetz, Jr.

Michigan

Ferguson Hospital
72 Sheldon Avenue, S. E.
Grand Rapids, MI 49503
(616) 456-0202
Program Director: Dr. W. Patrick Mazier

Henry Ford Hospital
2799 West Grand Boulevard
Detroit, MI 48202
(313) 876-2600
Program Director: Dr. Thomas Fox, Jr.

Minnesota

Mayo Clinic
200 S. W. First Street
Rochester, MN 55905
(507) 284-2511
Program Director: Dr. Roger R. Dozois

University of Minnesota Hospitals
Harvard Street at East River Road
Minneapolis, MN 55455
(612) 626-3000
Program Director: Dr. Stanley Goldberg

Missouri

Jewish Hospital of St. Louis
216 South Kingshighway Boulevard
St. Louis, MO 63110
(314) 454-7000
Program Director: Dr. Robert Fry

New Jersey

Muhlenberg Hospital
Park Avenue and Randolph Road
Plainfield, NJ 07061
(201) 668-1000
Program Director: Dr. Eugene Salvati

New York   Buffalo General Hospital
                    100 High Street
                    Buffalo, NY 14203
                    (716) 845-5600
                    Program Director: Dr. Amarjit Singh

Ohio   Cleveland Clinic Foundation
                    9500 Euclid Avenue
                    Cleveland, OH 44106
                    (216) 444-2200
                    Program Director: Ian C. Lavery

Pennsylvania   Lehigh Valley Hospital Center
                    1200 South Cedar Crest Boulevard
                    Allentown, PA 18185
                    (215) 776-8000
                    Program Director: Dr. Indru T. Khubchandani

                    Thomas Jefferson University Hospital
                    11th and Walnut Streets
                    Philadelphia, PA 19107
                    (215) 928-6000
                    Program Director: Dr. Gerald Marks

Texas   Baylor University Medical Center
                    3500 Gaston Avenue
                    Dallas, TX 75246
                    (214) 820-0111
                    Program Director: Dr. Wallace Bailey

DERMATOLOGIC SURGERY
(see also chapter 3, "Medicine")

Almost anyone who lives in or spends time in the Sun Belt region of the country is by now well aware of the ravages of the sun on the human skin. Former sun worshipers, now crowding dermatologists' waiting rooms to have skin cancers removed, are learning to forego the glorious tans they had once sought so avidly. But those crowded waiting rooms are also a result of a wide number of other skin conditions (notably adolescent acne, psoriasis, minor burns, and hard-to-heal wounds) that are usually treated by the dermatologist in his or her office.

Because most dermatologists perform skin surgery in their own offices, the importance of selecting a physician with the proper credentials as to training, local reputation, and knowledgeable skill is obvious. Your personal physician may guide you, but for the patient suffering from serious skin problems, the nearest teaching hospitals might well be the best bet.

Alabama	University of Alabama Medical Center 619 South 19th/University Station Birmingham, AL 35294 (205) 934-4141 Program Director: Dr. W. Mitchell Sams, Jr.
Arizona	University of Arizona Health Sciences Center 1501 North Campbell Avenue Tucson, AZ 85724 (602) 626-0111 Program Director: Dr. Peter Lynch
California	Stanford University Medical Center 300 Pasteur Drive Stanford, CA 94305 (415) 723-4000 Program Director: Dr. Eugene A. Bauer University of California San Francisco Hospitals and Clinics 505 Parnassus Avenue San Francisco, CA 94143 (415) 476-1000 Program Director: Dr. Bruce Wintroub (Special interest: allergic dermatitis)
Colorado	University of Colorado Health Sciences Center 4200 East Ninth Avenue Denver, CO 80262 (303) 329-3066 Program Director: Dr. William Weston
Connecticut	Yale–New Haven Hospital 333 Cedar Street New Haven, CT 06510 (203) 785-4242 Program Director: Dr. Aaron Lerner
Florida	University of Miami Affiliated Hospitals 1475 N. W. 12th Avenue Miami, FL 33136 (305) 547-6418 Program Director: Dr. William Eaglstein (Special interest: fungal infections)

Georgia   Emory University Hospital
                       1364 Clifton Road, N. E.
                       Atlanta, GA 30322
                       (404) 727-7021
                       Program Directors: Dr. Henry Jones
                                          Dr. Robert Rietschel

Illinois   Northwestern Memorial Hospital
                       250 East Superior Street
                       Chicago, IL 60611
                       (312) 908-8173
                       Program Director: Dr. Henry Roenigk, Jr.

                       University of Illinois Hospital
                       1740 West Taylor Street
                       Chicago, IL 60612
                       (312) 996-3000
                       Program Director: Dr. Lawrence Solomon

Minnesota   University of Minnesota Hospital
                       Harvard Street at East River Road
                       Minneapolis, MN 55455
                       (612) 626-3000
                       Program Director: Dr. Robert Goltz

                       Mayo Clinic
                       200 S. W. First Street
                       Rochester, MN 55905
                       (507) 284-2511
                       Program Director: Dr. Sigfrid Muller

New York   New York University Medical Center
                       First Avenue and 27th Street
                       New York, NY 10016
                       (212) 340-5505
                       Program Director: Dr. Irwin Freedberg

North Carolina   Duke University Medical Center
                       Box 3005
                       Durham, NC 22710
                       (919) 684-5587
                       Program Director: Dr. Sheldon Pinnell

Ohio   Cleveland Clinic Foundation
                       9500 Euclid Avenue
                       Cleveland, OH 44106
                       (216) 444-2200
                       Program Director: Dr. Phillip Ballin

Pennsylvania	Hospital of the University of Pennsylvania 3400 Spruce Street Philadelphia, PA 19104 (215) 662-6534 Program Director: Leonard M. Dzubow (Special interest: skin microbiology)
	University Health Center of Pittsburgh 121 Meyran Avenue Pittsburgh, PA 15260 (412) 647-2345 Program Director: Dr. Brian B. Jegasothy
Texas	Baylor College of Medicine and Hospitals One Baylor Plaza Houston, TX 77030 (713) 798-4951 Program Director: Dr. Michael Jarratt (Special interest: infectious skin diseases)
Virginia	Medical College of Virginia Hospital 401 North 12th Street Richmond, VA 23219 (804) 786-0932 Program Director: Dr. W. Kenneth Blaylock
Wisconsin	University of Wisconsin Hospitals and Clinics 600 Highland Avenue Madison, WI 53792 (608) 263-6230 Program Director: Dr. Derek J. Cripps

NEUROLOGICAL SURGERY
(see also chapter 3, "Medicine")

Among the concerns of the neurosurgeon are a variety of conditions involving the brain, the spinal cord, and the peripheral nerves, including traumatic injuries, abnormalities of the blood vessels, deficiencies in cerebrospinal fluid production and circulation, tumors, convulsive disorders, and the surgical relief of unbearable pain.

Advances in the basic sciences as applicable to neurological surgery, refined and minimally invasive imaging techniques, and the teamwork of surgeons, anesthetists, and radiologists—all are contributing to earlier and more precise diagnoses of disorders of the nervous system as well as to earlier, more complete, and less disruptive surgery. Certain conditions that just a few years ago were inoperable have now come within the realm of very successful treatment.

In some types of tumors, computerized tomographic (CT) and magnetic resonance (MR) scanners can distinguish abnormal from normal tissue far better than can the surgeon's eye, thus enabling the surgeon to do a more thorough job than would otherwise be possible. A powerful new piece of neurosurgical equipment called a gamma knife is now in operation in five U.S. medical centers. It uses precisely focused beams of radiation to destroy deep-seated inoperable brain masses, and it avoids the surgical risks of bleeding and postoperative infection.

A set of conditions involving the blood supply to the brain and spinal cord, called aneurysms, pose difficult problems for the neurosurgeon. Weakness of vessel walls causes outpouching along the course of a vessel or at junctures of vessels; leakage of blood may occur, or the sac may suddenly rupture. Although some aneurysms clot either spontaneously or when aided by the injection of clotting agents, they tend to recur and are associated with a high degree of mortality. The long controversy about the timing of an operation seems definitely to have been settled in favor of early. Use of the surgical microscope and, sometimes, a laser beam greatly facilitates surgery on small blood vessels.

Spinal injury and disease constitute other areas that may be helped by neurological surgery, which tends now to be less invasive than it once was. A common problem is spinal disk disease. A disk, which is a cushionlike structure that prevents two vertebrae from grating against each other, can degenerate or malfunction (slip out of position) and cause pressure on nerve roots, resulting in severe pain. One method of treatment, in which an enzyme (chymopapain) is injected to dissolve the disk, is not much in favor now because it is only about 40 percent successful, owing partly to complications that seem unrelated to the surgeon's technique and experience. For some disk cases, however, a new method, which involves a 2-millimeter suction and cutting instrument, seems quite promising, with only a few cases requiring repetition or other types of surgery for relief.

Research into the physiology of pain has resulted in increased ability to locate within the brain smaller receptor areas associated with consciousness of pain and to approach them surgically. Many patients are thereby relieved of pain without the necessity of taking drugs that depress vital functions and other areas of consciousness.

In this brief survey, we must mention a relatively new technique that involves the grafting of nerve cells often obtained from fetal tissues. The basic research, which may eventually benefit a number of nervous system diseases, is not yet developed enough, particularly with respect to understanding pathways of action, to warrant use of such transplants in humans for the treatment of Parkinson's disease. Even apart from ethical considerations, the mortality rate of such operations seems unacceptably high.

The odds for the favorable outcome of a neurosurgical procedure improve tremendously when the patient has early access to an institution of recognized skill and vast experience. All the centers we have listed are competent within the entire field, but we have further indicated those with special expertise in one or more subdivisions of this specialty.

Alabama	University of Alabama Medical Center 619 South 19th Street/University Station Birmingham, AL 35294 (205) 934-7170 Program Director: Dr. Richard B. Morowetz
California	University of California San Francisco Hospitals and Clinics 505 Parnassus Avenue San Francisco, CA 94143 (415) 476-1000 Program Director: Dr. Charles Wilson (Special interest: brain microsurgery)
Connecticut	University of Connecticut Health Center 263 Farmington Avenue Farmington, CT 06032 (203) 674-2000 Program Director: Dr. Richard H. Simon (Special interest: spinal surgery)
Florida	Shands Hospital—University of Florida 1600 S. W. Archer Road Gainesville, FL 32610 (904) 392-4331 Program Director: Dr. Albert Rhoton, Jr. (Special interests: brain, spinal, and pediatric neurosurgery)
Illinois	University of Illinois Hospital 1740 West Taylor Street Chicago, IL 60612 (312) 996-3000 Program Director: Dr. Robert Crowell
Louisiana	Alton Ochsner Medical Foundation 1516 Jefferson Highway New Orleans, LA 70121 (504) 838-3000 Program Director: Dr. David Kline

Maryland	Johns Hopkins Hospital 600 North Wolfe Street Baltimore, MD 21205 (301) 955-5000 Program Director: Dr. James N. Campbell (Special interests: vascular and pediatric neurosurgery and pain research)
Massachusetts	Massachusetts General Hospital 32 Fruit Street Boston, MA 02114 (617) 726-2000 Program Director: Dr. Nicholas Zervas (Special interests: vascular and pituitary neurosurgery)
Michigan	University of Michigan Hospitals 1500 East Medical Center Drive Ann Arbor, MI 48109 (313) 936-4000 Program Director: Dr. Julian Hoff
Minnesota	Mayo Clinic 200 S. W. First Street Rochester, MN 55905 (507) 284-2511 Program Director: Dr. Thoralf Sundt, Jr. (Special interests: vascular and pituitary neurosurgery)
New Hampshire	Dartmouth-Hitchcock Medical Center 2 Maynard Street Hanover, NH 03756 (603) 646-5000 Program Director: Dr. Richard Saunders
New York	New York Hospital–Cornell Medical Center 525 East 68th Street New York, NY 10021 (212) 746-5454 Program Director: Dr. Russell Patterson, Jr. (Special interest: tumor neurosurgery) Neurological Institute, Columbia-Presbyterian Medical Center 710 West 168th Street New York, NY 10032 (212) 694-2500 Program Director: Dr. Bennett Stein

New York University Medical Center
First Avenue and 27th Street
New York, NY 10016
(212) 340-5505
Program Director: Dr. Joseph Ransohoff
(Special interest: spinal surgery)

North Carolina   Duke University Medical Center
Box 3807
Durham, NC 27710
(919) 684-5587
Program Director: Dr. Robert H. Wilkins

Ohio   University of Cincinnati Hospital
234 Goodman Street
Cincinnati, OH 45267
(513) 558-1000
Program Director: Dr. John Tew
(Special interests: carotid artery and tumor surgery)

Pennsylvania   Hospital of the University of Pennsylvania
3400 Spruce Street
Philadelphia, PA 19104
(215) 662-3483
Program Director: Eugene S. Flamm

Presbyterian-University Hospital
De Sota and O'Hara Streets
Pittsburgh, PA 15213
(412) 647-2345
Program Director: Dr. Peter J. Jannetta

Texas   Methodist Hospital
6516 Bertner Drive
Houston, TX 77030
(713) 790-3311
Program Director: Dr. Robert Grossman

Utah   University of Utah Medical Center
50th North Medical Drive
Salt Lake City, UT 84132
(801) 581-6908
Program Director: Dr. M. Peter Heilbrun
(Special interests: artificial limbs and limb reattachment)

Washington   University of Washington Medical Center
                                1959 N. E. Pacific Street
                                Seattle, WA 98195
                                (206) 543-3570
                                Program Director: Dr. H. Richard Winn
                                (Special interest: convulsive disorders)

OBSTETRICS/GYNECOLOGY

In its broadest sense, obstetrics/gynecology is both the medicine and the surgery
of the female reproductive organs; as such, it interacts with virtually all the other
specialties. Among its concerns are endocrinology and fertility problems, the
management of normal and abnormal pregnancies, reconstructive surgery, the
surgery of tumors, and the prevention of cancer.

Many women today desire natural childbirth without heavy sedation and
anesthetics, either in their homes or in the hospital. Physicians have been quick
to see some of the advantages of natural childbirth for uncomplicated pregnancies and for labors that can be expected to proceed without unusual risk to mother
or baby. Even with these preconditions, there is an increased element of risk,
slight though it may be, in having a baby outside the delivery room of a hospital.
Unexpected, sometimes serious, complications may occur at any stage of labor.
Hospitals have been trying to accommodate patients' desires for a homelike
atmosphere insofar as possible. Many obstetricians encourage the participation
of the father in the labor and delivery rooms.

Selecting your obstetrician early in pregnancy is an important step. If you are
consulting a group of obstetricians (group practice in this specialty is quite
usual), you must be sure of the group's policies regarding attendance for prenatal
examinations, especially concerning whether you must accept whoever is on call
the day of your delivery. Ask about their policies of inducing labor at term versus
allowing natural labor. There are, indeed, good medical reasons for induction of
labor, but the doctor's or hospital's convenience is not one of them. It is, of
course, important that you feel confident and comfortable with your doctor and
his or her associates.

There is considerable concern about the cesarean-section rate in some hospitals. Excluding the statistics for high-risk obstetrical units—where the rate is
expected to be higher—the rate of some hospitals is over 30 percent, which is far
too high. Ask about the rate for your obstetrician and the rate for the hospital.
This is a fairly reliable objective index of quality care. If it is much over 15
percent, you will probably wish to seek other care.

Increasingly, labors that are anticipated to be riskier than average for the
mother, baby, or both, are conducted in hospitals that have special units designed
both for coping with a difficult labor and for a rapid change of plans, as the safety
of the mother or the baby indicates. In such units a cesarean section can be
started within 10 or 15 minutes—anesthetists are present in the hospital, not

merely on call, pediatricians specializing in neonatal care are immediately available, and laboratories function as well at 3:00 A.M. as they do at noon. Some of the conditions best treated in such hospital units are toxemias of pregnancy; care for mothers with heart disease, diabetes, or bleeding problems; oversized or undersized babies; untoward positions of the baby; and the delivery of newborns with congenital anomalies recognized or suspected before birth. Also, under these special hospital conditions, it is now safe to allow some women who have had a previous cesarean section to deliver normally.

The increasing ability to help childless couples who want offspring is surely one of the brightest aspects of modern obstetrics/gynecology. Although it is true that many such couples are eventually helped to successful fertility by attention to the general health of both partners or to the correction of problems (hormonal imbalances, anatomical abnormalities, infections, psychological factors) in one or both, there are still quite a number whose infertility has obscure causes. For these couples, embryo transfer, pioneered by the British and Australians might be recommended. The first live baby conceived by this method in the United States was born late in 1981; worldwide, more than 200 such births have occurred since. The method, a tedious one, involves controlled laboratory procedures at each step. Ripening of the ovum (egg) on the surface of the ovary is encouraged by imitating nature's hormonal balance as far as possible; at the right time the egg is lifted, placed in a special test tube, and incubated. Some hours later, fresh sperm is introduced under controlled conditions. Fertilization then occurs. About 22 hours later the fertilized egg is introduced into the uterus. Implantation is the most crucial step; it is not known exactly how this occurs naturally, and only about 20 percent of such fertilized eggs thrive and grow. Although not all eggs survive, researchers anticipate that in the not-too-distant future as many as 30 percent of infertile couples will be able to have a child through this method.

In recent years, scientific knowledge of human fertility and reproduction has encouraged a rapid rise in the number of fertility specialists and in-vitro fertilization clinics, and in the number of childless couples seeking help. The American Fertility Society seeks to provide help upon the request of physicians or those seeking information. Originally begun in 1944 (the same year as the American Society for the Study of Sterility), the society now lists some 8,000 members, including obstetricians, gynecologists, reproductive endocrinologists, urologists, and other specialists from every state and over 75 countries. An active public education service develops and maintains physician-scientist channels of information and directs patients to the most appropriate source of help, including to specialists throughout the United States and abroad. The society also furnishes physicians and patients with information booklets on any aspect of the reproductive system for nominal fees (from $1 to $5 or more for technical studies designed for the medical profession). In addition, the American Fertility Society furnishes a complete list of hospitals and medical centers in the United States that accept referrals to and engage in in-vitro fertilization programs. For more information contact:

American Fertility Society
2131 Magnolia Avenue
Birmingham, AL 35256
(205) 251-9764

Breast and cervical cancer are being drastically reduced through regularly scheduled clinical examinations by gynecologists and by laboratory tests of cellular by-products. More cases are now being diagnosed while in very early stages, often as a result of suspicions about small changes in appearance that were once thought to be associated with benign conditions. For example, changes associated with two types of viruses—herpes-2 and papilloma—are also found in a high percentage of proven cases of certain types of cancer, although neither virus has been proven a direct cause.

New techniques of general surgery now apply to gynecologic surgery, permitting much more extensive surgical resectioning of tumor-bearing areas than was formerly possible. Improved methods of radiation are saving more women's lives, as is chemotherapy management when indicated for some types of malignant tumors. Nothing is more important in preventing cancer, however, than periodic, thorough examinations, even when there are no symptoms of trouble.

Alabama   University of South Alabama Medical Center
                   2451 Fillingim Street
                   Mobile, AL 36617
                   (205) 471-7000
                   Program Director: Dr. Hiram Mendenhall
                   (Special interests: fertility problems, endocrinology)

Arizona   University of Arizona Health Sciences Center
                   1501 North Campbell Avenue
                   Tucson, AZ 85724
                   (602) 626-0111
                   Program Director: Dr. C. D. Christian

California   University of California Irvine Medical Center
                   101 City Drive, South
                   Orange, CA 92668
                   (714) 634-5678
                   Program Director: Dr. Thomas J. Garite
                   (Special interests: fertility problems, high-risk pregnancy, cancer surgery)

                   University of California Los Angeles Medical Center
                   10833 Le Conte Avenue
                   Los Angeles, CA 90024
                   (213) 825-9111
                   Program Director: Dr. Roy M. Pitkin
                   (Special interests: fertility problems, high-risk pregnancy, cancer surgery)

Connecticut	Yale–New Haven Hospital 333 Cedar Street New Haven, CT 06510 (203) 785-4242 Program Director: Dr. Frederick Naftolin (Special interests: fertility problems, cancer surgery, high-risk pregnancy)
District of Columbia	Georgetown University Hospital 3800 Reservoir Road, N. W. Washington, DC 20007 (202) 625-7001 Program Director: Dr. John T. Queenan (Special interest: high-risk pregnancy)
Florida	University of Miami Affiliated Hospitals 1475 N. W. 12th Avenue Miami, FL 33136 (305) 549-6944 Program Director: Dr. William Little (Special interests: high-risk pregnancy, cancer surgery, fertility programs)
Illinois	Prentice Women's Hospital and Maternity Center 250 East Superior Street Chicago, IL 30311 (312) 908-7504 Program Director: Dr. John Sciarra (Special interests: high-risk pregnancy, surgical gynecology)
Iowa	University of Iowa Hospitals and Clinics 650 Newton Road Iowa City, IA 52242 (319) 356-1976 Program Director: Dr. J. R. Niebyl (Special interest: high-risk pregnancy)
Maryland	University of Maryland Medical Systems 22 South Greene Street Baltimore, MD 21201 (301) 328-6640 Program Director: Dr. Carlyle Crenshaw, Jr. (Special interest: high-risk pregnancy)

Massachusetts Brigham and Women's Hospital
75 Francis Street
Boston, MA 02115
(617) 732-5500
Program Director: Dr. Kenneth Ryan
(Special interests: fertility problems, high-risk pregnancy)

Michigan University of Michigan Hospitals
1500 East Medical Center Drive
Ann Arbor, MI 48109
(313) 936-4000
Program Director: Dr. Preston V. Ditts, Jr.
(Special interests: fertility problems, cancer surgery)

Mississippi University Hospital
2500 North State Street
Jackson, MS 39216
(601) 987-4811
Program Director: Dr. Winfred Wiser
(Special interests: high-risk pregnancy, cancer surgery)

New York Mt. Sinai Hospital
One Gustav Levy Place
New York, NY 10029
(212) 650-6500
Program Director: Dr. Richard Berkowitz
(Special interests: fertility problems, cancer surgery)

Ohio Ohio State University Hospitals
410 West Tenth Avenue
Columbus, OH 43210
(614) 421-8000
Program Director: Dr. Steven G. Gobbe
(Special interests: fertility problems, high-risk pregnancy)

Pennsylvania Hospital of the University of Pennsylvania
3400 Spruce Street
Philadelphia, PA 19104
(215) 662-6037
Program Director: Dr. Michael T. Mennuti
(Special interests: fertility problems, high-risk pregnancy, cancer surgery)

Tennessee	Vanderbilt University Hospital 1211 22nd Avenue, S. W. Nashville, TN 37232 (615) 322-7311 Program Director: Dr. Lonnie Burnett (Special interest: cancer surgery)
Texas	Parkland Memorial Hospital 5201 Harry Hines Boulevard Dallas, TX 75235 (214) 590-8000 Program Director: Dr. Kenneth Leveno (Special interests: high-risk pregnancy, fertility problems)
Virginia	University of Virginia Hospital Jefferson Park Avenue Charlottesville, VA 22908 (804) 924-0211 Program Director: Dr. Paul Underwood (Special interests: high-risk pregnancy, cancer surgery)

OPHTHALMIC SURGERY

Few parts of the body have been the object of more thorough study from so many different aspects than the human eye. Application of the sciences of chemistry, physics, physiology, embryology, histology, and pharmacology to the study of various tissues of the eye have led to the prevention of some causes of blindness and to the improvement and restoration of vision for many patients. So much knowledge has accumulated about this small but important organ that, far from being combined with ear, nose, and throat diseases as was usual in the early part of this century, ophthalmology has itself become subdivided into several areas of particular interest: studies of the cornea; the diseases of glaucoma and cataracts (involving the anterior portion of the eye); retinal diseases and vitreous disorders (involving the posterior chamber of the eye); diseases of the ocular muscles and the eyelids; and neuro-ophthalmology. Neuro-ophthalmology is important in the diagnosis of some brain tumors, because the optic-nerve fibers run from the eye to the back of the brain along fairly well-known pathways.

Ophthalmology also has important connection with general medicine. For example, diabetes, certain diseases of the liver and kidneys, and hypertension may first be diagnosed through an examination of the eye, where their effects can easily be seen through the ophthalmoscope. Improved photography of the interior of the eye has advanced the studies of both eye diseases and of general diseases that affect the eye.

Glaucomas of several types involve pressure of accumulated ocular fluid in the anterior part of the eye. Discovered early in its course, it can be controlled in the great majority of cases with noninvasive medical treatment. Where medical treatment is not entirely effective, surgery may be necessary. Laser beams can now be directed on congested outflow channels to treat glaucoma when medical measures have failed.

Cataract surgery has gone through a number of recent changes. Artificial lens implants, for instance, have been technically improved to most patients' satisfaction, although complications do occur, and the long-term effects are still being assessed. Retinal surgery has also undergone many advances in the past 35 years. In cases of detached retinas, surgeons are now quite experienced in the procedures for reattaching and mending holes in the retina, and keeping the retina in place. Before this knowledge, patients would often lay on their backs while everyone hoped nature would reattach the retina. Hospitalization has been reduced from weeks to usually a day or two for this condition.

Other advancements in this field include cornea transplants, operations to correct muscle imbalances, tear-sac surgery, and plastic surgery for eyelid abnormalities or the masking of the results of eye injury.

Alabama

University of Alabama Medical Center
619 South 19th Street/University Station
Birmingham, AL 35294
(205) 934-2014
Program Director: Dr. Harold Skalka

California

Jules Stein Eye Institute
800 Westwood Plaza
Los Angeles, CA 90024
(213) 825-8556
Program Director: Dr. Bradley Straatsma
(Special interest: retina surgery)

University of California San Diego Medical Center
225 Dickinson Street
San Diego, CA 92103
(619) 294-6222
Program Director: Dr. Stuart I. Brown
(Special interest: cornea surgery)

District of
Columbia

George Washington University Hospital
901 23rd Street, N. W.
Washington, DC 20037
(202) 994-1000
Program Director: Dr. Mansour Armaly

Florida	Bascom Palmer Eye Institute Anne Bates Leach Eye Hospital 900 N. W. 17th Street Miami, FL 33136 (305) 326-6032 Program Director: Dr. Edward W. D. Norton (Special interests: retina, cornea, cataract, and glaucoma surgery)
Georgia	Emory University Hospital 1364 Clifton Road, N. E. Atlanta, GA 30322 (404) 321-0111 Program Director: Dr. William Coles
Illinois	University of Illinois Eye and Ear Infirmary 1855 West Taylor Street Chicago, IL 60612 (312) 996-6536 Program Director: Dr. Morton Goldberg
Iowa	University of Iowa Hospitals and Clinics 650 Newton Road Iowa City, IA 52242 (319) 356-2867 Program Director: T. A. Weingeist (Special interests: cornea and retina surgery)
Maryland	Johns Hopkins Hospital—Wilmer Eye Institute 600 North Wolfe Street Baltimore, MD 21205 (301) 955-5000 Program Director: Dr. Arnall Patz (Special interests: retina and cataract surgery)
Massachusetts	Massachusetts Eye and Ear Infirmary 243 Charles Street Boston, MA 02114 (617) 522-8110 Program Director: Dr. Frank Berson (Special interests: cornea, retina, and cataract surgery)
New York	New York Hospital–Cornell Medical Center 525 East 68th Street New York, NY 10021 (212) 746-5454 Program Director: Dr. D. Jackson Coleman

Columbia-Presbyterian Medical Center
622 West 168th Street
New York, NY 10032
(212) 305-2500
Program Director: Dr. Charles Campbell

North Carolina   Duke Eye Center
Duke University Medical Center
Box 3005
Durham, NC 27710
(919) 684-5587
Program Director: Dr. James Tiedeman
(Special interests: retina surgery, tumor treatment)

Ohio   Case Western Reserve University Hospital
2145 Adelbert Road
Cleveland, OH 44016
(216) 368-2450
Program Director: Dr. E. W. Purnell

Pennsylvania   Wills Eye Hospital
Ninth and Walnut Streets
Philadelphia, PA 19107
(215) 928-3000
Program Director: Dr. John Jeffers

Scheie Eye Institute—University of Pennsylvania
51 North 39th Street
Philadelphia, PA 19104
(215) 662-8715
Program Director: Dr. Theodore Krupin

Eye and Ear Hospital of Pittsburgh
230 Lothrop Street
Pittsburgh, PA 15213
(412) 647-2010
Program Director: Dr. Richard A. Thoft

Wisconsin   University of Wisconsin Hospital and Clinics
600 Highland Avenue
Madison, WI 53792
(608) 263-6070
Program Director: Dr. John W. Chandler

ORTHOPEDIC SURGERY

The word *orthopedics* comes from two Greek words which, taken together, mean "straight child"; this reflects its beginnings as a specialty dealing mainly with deformities of children. In fact, it was the first of all pediatric specialties, developed long before general pediatric surgery. Of course, it has expanded to include all age groups with diseases, injuries, and deformities of the musculoskeletal system. As with other specialties, more or less overlapping fields of special interest have developed: trauma, fracture, spinal diseases, deformities, hand surgery, joint replacement, pediatric orthopedics, and sports medicine.

The diagnosis and treatment of many orthopedic conditions have been advanced by a number of technological developments, including CAT scanning, which gives a three-dimensional picture of anatomical structures; arthroscopy, which allows visualization of the interior of joints; the development of microsurgical instruments; and the electronic monitoring of nerve functions during operations.

Microsurgery of blood vessels, nerves, tendons, and other tissues has been of tremendous help in saving limbs that have sustained severe injury. In some cases, the reattachment of completely severed limbs has been made possible by "replant" teams of surgeons now operating in many large medical centers.

Joint replacement surgery, first performed successfully on the hip in the early 1970s, is presently capable of replacing all joints. Problems are encountered at times: loosening of the prosthetic materials, incompatibility of some types of materials with the patient's tissues, and problems occasioned by the natural growth of young people who have submitted to joint replacement procedures. A number of these problems are now being solved through laboratory work and by improved technical procedures.

Exaggerated spinal curvature, a condition known as scoliosis, is being identified much earlier than it has ever been. A combination of treatments using exercise, electrical stimulation of certain muscles during sleep, and braces has made surgery necessary in only about one-third of the cases for which it was formerly advised. New methods of wiring the vertebrae, when necessary, help avoid the discomfort of cumbersome braces.

The process of forming new bone—which must occur for fractures to heal—has been hastened by new methods of setting the fragments and allowing for limited motion, by electrical stimulation and by the use of pulsating magnetic fields, which promote calcium deposition around the break.

For most orthopedic conditions, especially those in children, there are numerous nonsurgical methods of treatment that should be given ample trial before resorting to surgical procedures that may be of questionable value. Most informed foreign doctors observing the American medical scene feel that American doctors place far too much emphasis upon invasive methods of treatment. It is difficult to counter these views when we know, for example, that a certain operation for spinal-disk disease is ten times more frequent in certain parts of the United States than it is in Great Britain. Thus, it is important to seek care in a center that offers a number of treatment options and that has a variety of personnel who are knowledgeable about their indications and uses.

Alabama	University of South Alabama Medical Center 2451 Fillingim Street Mobile, AL 36617 (205) 471-7000 Program Director: Dr. Lewis Anderson (Special interest: fractures)
Arkansas	University Hospital and Ambulatory Care Center 4301 West Markham Street Little Rock, AR 72205 (501) 686-5000 Program Director: Dr. Carl Nelson (Special interest: arthritis surgery)
California	University of Southern California Medical Center 1200 North State Street Los Angeles, CA 90033 (213) 226-2345 Program Director: Dr. Augusto Sarmienta
	St. Mary's Hospital and Medical Center 450 Stanyan Street San Francisco, CA 94117 (415) 221-0665 Program Director: Dr. Richard Welch
Delaware	Alfred I. Dupont Institute Box 269, Rockland Road Wilmington, DE 19899 (302) 651-4000 Program Director: Dr. William Bunnell (Special interests: spine, hip, and foot abnormalities)
Florida	Nemours Children's Clinic 841 Prudential Drive Jacksonville, FL 32207 (904) 390-3600 Program Director: Dr. R. J. Cummings (Special interests: children's orthopedics as related to the spine, hip, foot, cerebral palsy, and neurologic diseases)
Georgia	Georgia Baptist Medical Center 300 Boulevard, N. E. Atlanta, GA 30312 (404) 653-4200 Program Director: Dr. Lee Cross

Scottish Rite Children's Hospital
1001 Johnson Ferry Road, N. E.
Atlanta, GA 30363
(404) 256-5252
Program Director: Dr. Raymond T. Morrissy
(Special interests: spine, hip, and foot abnormalities)

Illinois

Rush-Presbyterian-St. Luke's Medical Center
1653 West Congress Parkway
Chicago, IL 60612
(312) 942-5850
Program Director: Dr. Ken N. Kuo
(Special interest: joint replacement)

Southern Illinois University School of Medicine
801 North Rutledge
P. O. Box 19230
Springfield, IL 62794
(217) 782-8864
Program Director: Dr. E. Shannon Stauffer

Indiana

Indiana University Medical Center, Department of
    Orthopedic Surgery
926 West Michigan Street
Indianapolis, IN 46223
(317) 924-6411
Program Director: Dr. G. Paul De Rosa
(Special interest: arthritis surgery)

Iowa

University of Iowa Hospitals and Clinics
650 Newton Road
Iowa City, IA 52242
(319) 356-3470
Program Director: Dr. Reginald Cooper
(Special interests: joint replacement, children's
    orthopedics, metabolic disorders, neuromuscular
    diseases)

Maryland

Johns Hopkins Hospital
600 North Wolfe Street
Baltimore, MD 21205
(301) 955-5000
Program Director: Dr. Lee Riley, Jr.
(Special interest: joint replacement)

Massachusetts	Massachusetts General Hospital
	32 Fruit Street
	Boston, MA 02114
	(617) 726-2000
	Program Director: Dr. Henry Mankin
	(Special interests: fracture, trauma, joint replacement, children's orthopedics)

Massachusetts

Massachusetts General Hospital
32 Fruit Street
Boston, MA 02114
(617) 726-2000
Program Director: Dr. Henry Mankin
(Special interests: fracture, trauma, joint replacement, children's orthopedics)

Minnesota

Mayo Clinic
200 S. W. First Street
Rochester, MN 55905
(507) 284-2511
Program Director: Dr. Bernard F. Morrey
(Special interests: reconstructive surgery, joint replacement, children's orthopedics)

New Hampshire

Dartmouth-Hitchcock Medical Center
2 Maynard Street
Hanover, NH 03756
(603) 646-5000
Program Director: Dr. Michael B. Mayor
(Special interests: spinal cord injuries, sports medicine)

New York

Hospital for Special Surgery
535 East 70th Street
New York, NY 10021
(212) 606-1000
Program Director: Dr. Philip Wilson, Jr.
(Special interests: joint replacement, reconstructive surgery; a multipurpose arthritis center)

Oregon

Oregon Health Sciences University Hospital
3181 West Sam Jackson Park Road
Portland, OR 97201
(503) 225-8311
Program Director: Dr. Rodney Beals

Pennsylvania

Thomas Jefferson University Hospital
11th and Walnut Streets
Philadelphia, PA 19107
(215) 928-6000
Program Director: Dr. Richard H. Rothman

Presbyterian-University Hospital
De Sota and O'Hara Streets
Pittsburgh, PA 15213
(412) 647-2345
Program Director: Dr. Albert Ferguson, Jr.
(Special interests: sports medicine, joint reconstruction)

Tennessee

Campbell Clinic of the University of Tennessee
869 Madison Avenue
Memphis, TN 38104
(901) 525-2531
Program Director: Dr. Edward N. Hanley, Jr.
(Special interests: joint replacement, arthritis surgery, children's orthopedics, fractures, and trauma)

OTOLARYNGOLOGY

Few specialties have been more changed than otolaryngology by the continuing development of antimicrobial drugs. Formerly, ear, nose, and throat (ENT) specialists' time was taken up largely in the treatment of acute and chronic infections of the ear, mastoid, sinuses, throat, and upper respiratory passages, as well as the treatment of their sometimes life-threatening complications: meningitis, brain abscess, osteomyelitis, and so on. As antimicrobial drugs have curtailed the number and severity of these cases, there has been time to study and treat other diseases that were more or less neglected—for example, noninfectious causes of deafness and dizziness. Antimicrobial drugs have also facilitated more extensive tumor surgery, and plastic and reconstructive surgery of the head and neck. Emphasis is now not only on adequate removal of disease but also on improvement and restoration of function wherever possible.

Surgery of the middle ear has been advanced to a high degree of perfection by the development of the operating microscope and microsurgical instruments, permitting most operations to be accomplished by incisions within the ear canal. Where there is destruction by disease of middle ear structures, which serve to conduct sound to the inner ear, the implantation of facsimiles of these structures restores unaided hearing in many patients.

Otosclerosis, a disease of unknown cause, is a common cause of deafness. Surgery, in suitable cases, is the only successful treatment of it. Attention is directed primarily to the stapes, the smallest of the three middle ear bones, which becomes "frozen" and therefore unable to conduct sound to the inner ear. Operations on this structure have been brought to a high degree of perfection by the principles established by Dr. John Shea of Memphis, the American pioneer of this surgery who has performed more than 35,000 stapes operations. Although many otolaryngologists include microsurgery of the ear among their varied interests within the entire field, a patient requiring such surgery is well advised to seek out the surgeon whose work is limited to otology and otological surgery. The reason is that the surgery varies in difficulty from patient to patient, and the difficult cases cannot usually be predicted in advance of the operation. The necessity of a second operation will usually compromise the final hearing result.

Surgery of the previously described types depends for its success upon good functioning of the inner ear and its central connections. When the nerve elements do not function satisfactorily, the patient must rely upon a hearing aid. Hearing aids of sophisticated circuitry are available; some are computerized to screen out unwanted sounds. The help to be expected from a hearing aid or from surgery depends upon the patient's ability to discriminate speech sounds at a comfortable level of amplication. Most nerve-deaf patients are helped by a properly fitted hearing aid.

For the profoundly deaf patient who cannot wear a hearing aid satisfactorily, there is new help. The cochlear implant, developed by Dr. William House of the Otological Medical Group in Los Angeles, Dr. George Facer of the Mayo Clinic, and others, has clearly emerged as a suitable method of helping about 1 percent of the 16 million hearing-impaired people in the United States. This surgically implanted device, still being improved technically, is best suited to patients who have once had fairly serviceable hearing. It enables them to hear the sounds such as the slamming of doors, and telephone and alarm bells, thus bringing them into better contact with their environment. In some cases, speech discriminatory ability can be raised to the level required for successful use of a hearing aid or telephone.

Tumors of the auditory nerve connecting the inner ear with the brain are now being found while quite small, improved early diagnosis being due mainly to ABER (automated brain-stem evoked response test), an objective test of hearing designed to locate the region of the auditory pathway that is affected by disease; and more recently to magnetic resonance imaging (MRI) studies. If confined to the auditory canal, these tumors (which are malignant in the sense that they may, because of increasing size, encroach upon vital structures in the brain) can be removed by the otological surgeon, occasionally with preservation of hearing.

Treatment of inner ear diseases, medically or surgically, is not very advanced. Dizziness owing to inner ear causes may be abolished by surgical destruction of the labyrinthine portion of the inner ear, but usually not without untoward effects on hearing function. A new method, still in its investigative stages, in which streptomycin (a drug toxic to the balancing function but not to hearing) is perfused into the labyrinthine fluids, may turn out to be the best method for helping patients with Mèniére's type of vertigo.

A new method of surgical treatment, originating in Germany, of infectious sinusitis has been further developed in the United States within the past five years. It is called functional endoscopic sinus surgery and directs attention to the small, crowded areas of the lateral nasal wall where the sinuses drain. Fiberoptic endoscopes enable direct visualization of these affected areas as well as the interior (in most cases) of all the sinuses. Special instruments—some with lights on their tips—are used to remove secretions, diseased tissue, and where disease interferes with drainage from one or more of the sinuses. Accomplished under local anesthesia, usually on an out-patient basis, the method is associated with minimum unpleasant aftereffects, fewer complications, and a greatly reduced need for grossly invasive surgery upon the sinuses themselves. Results beginning to emerge from several long-term studies of this exacting method are indeed impressive.

Tumors of many types may involve the head and neck structures. When they first involve the mucous membrane areas of the nose, sinuses, and throat, as well as the larynx, they can as a rule easily be seen while quite small. The diagnosis of subsurface tumors is greatly helped by CAT-scan radiography and MRI. The outlook for surgical treatment of benign lesions and of malignant ones if diagnosed early is quite good. In addition, X ray and chemotherapy, alone or in conjunction with surgery, are salvaging more cases involving certain types of tumors. Coincidentally, with the improved ability to remove tumors more thoroughly than ever before, there has developed more complete understanding of the growth patterns of some malignant tumors, which allows more limited removal of surrounding tissues without increasing the risks of recurrence or spread. Such conservative operations facilitate restoration or preservation of vocal, respiratory, and swallowing functions in suitable cases. Laryngoscopes with improved methods of illumination, often with laser attachments, enable the more accurate removal of benign and malignant tumors from the vocal chords and other areas of the larynx and surrounding tissues.

Study of nerve-muscle functions involved in voice production by the healthy and the diseased larynx is being translated into specific methods of treatment for vocal impairments of several types. About 25 percent of patients who have had laryngectomies achieve good, sometimes quite remarkable, esophageal voices. For others, implantable valves of several types are being improved upon, while the goal of an implantable larynx is being steadily pursued by Dr. Harvey Tucker of the Cleveland Clinic.

California   University of California Los Angeles Medical Center
10833 Le Conte Avenue
Los Angeles, CA 90024
(213) 825-9111
Program Director: Dr. Paul Ward
(Special interests: head and neck surgery, voice disorders)

Otological Medical Group
2122 West Third Street
Los Angeles, CA 90057
(213) 483-9930
Program Director: Dr. James L. Sheehy
(Special interests: middle- and inner-ear surgery, acoustic-nerve tumors)

Florida   Jackson Memorial Hospital
                   1611 N. W. 12th Avenue
                   Miami, FL 33136
                   (305) 549-6101
                   Program Director: Dr. James Chandler

Illinois   Northwestern University Medical Center
                   250 East Superior Street
                   Chicago, IL 60611
                   (312) 908-8182
                   Program Director: Dr. George Sisson

Louisiana   Eye and Ear Institute
                   Tulane Medical Center Hospital and Clinics
                   1415 Tulane Avenue
                   New Orleans, LA 70112
                   (504) 588-5471
                   Program Director: Dr. Robert H. Miller

Maryland   Johns Hopkins Hospital
                   600 North Wolfe Street
                   Baltimore, MD 21205
                   (301) 955-5000
                   Program Director: Dr. Michael Johns
                   (Special interests: diseases of the ear, hearing disor-
                     ders)

Massachusetts   Massachusetts Eye and Ear Infirmary
                   243 Charles Street
                   Boston, MA 02114
                   (617) 523-7900
                   Program Director: Dr. Joseph Nadol
                   (Special interests: ear, sinus, head, and neck surgery:
                     hearing disorders)

                   Lahey Clinic Foundation
                   41 Mall Road
                   Burlington, MA 01805
                   (617) 273-8450
                   Program Director: Stanley M. Shapshay
                   (Special interests: laryngeal surgery, laser beam en-
                     doscopy of the upper and lower respiratory areas)

Minnesota   Minnesota Ear Head and Neck Clinic
                   701 25th Avenue South
                   Minneapolis, MN 55454
                   (612) 339-2836
                   Program Director: Michael M. Paparella

Mayo Clinic
200 S. W. First Street
Rochester, MN 55905
(507) 284-2511
Program Director: Dr. H. Bryan Neel III

Missouri

Barnes Hospital
One Barnes Plaza
St. Louis, MO 63110
(314) 362-7552
Program Director: Dr. John Fredrickson
(Special interests: head and neck tumors)

New York

Mt. Sinai Hospital
One Gustav Levy Place
New York, NY 10029
(212) 650-6500
Program Director: Dr. Hugh Biller
(Special interests: head and neck surgery, malignant
    tumors)

University Hospital—Upstate Medical Center
750 East Adams Street
Syracuse, NY 13210
(315) 473-5540
Program Director: Dr. Richard Gacek
(Special interests: voice disorders, ear surgery)

Ohio

Cleveland Clinic Foundation
9500 Euclid Avenue
Cleveland, OH 44106
(216) 444-2200
Program Director: Dr. Harvey Tucker
(Special interests: laryngeal reconstructive surgery,
    inner ear disorders)

Ohio State University Hospitals
410 West Tenth Avenue
Columbus, OH 43210
(614) 293-8150
Program Director: David E. Schuller

Pennsylvania

Eye and Ear Hospital of Pittsburgh
230 Lothrop Street
Pittsburgh, PA 15213
(412) 647-2010
Program Director: Dr. Eugene Meyers
(Special interests: head and neck surgery, facial nerve
    surgery)

Hospital of the University of Pennsylvania
3400 Spruce Street
Philadelphia, PA 19104
(215) 662-2654
Program Director: Dr. James B. Snow, Jr.

Tennessee   Shea Clinic (Otology)
6133 Poplar Pike at Ridgeway
Memphis, TN 38119
(901) 761-9720
Program Director: Dr. John Shea
(Special interests: diseases of the ear, ear surgery)

Texas   Baylor College of Medicine and Hospitals
One Baylor Plaza
Houston, TX 77030
(713) 798-4951
Program Director: Bobby R. Alford
(Special interests: neuro-otology, head and neck sur-
gery)

Washington   University of Washington Medical Center
1959 N. E. Pacific Street
Seattle, WA 98195
(206) 543-5230
Program Director: Dr. Charles Cummings

PEDIATRIC SURGERY
(see also chapter 9, "Pediatrics")

Surgery for the youngest of patients is also the newest of the surgical specialties.
Prior to 1945 most children's conditions requiring surgery were handled by
general surgeons, a few of whom had begun to emphasize the surgery of children
by modifying principles that were suitable for adults. More than in most other
specialties, the development and progress of pediatric surgery are due mainly to
one man's versatile capabilities and concern for the general welfare of children—
Dr. C. Everett Koop of Philadelphia, who, until recently, was the Surgeon
General of the United States. Dr. Koop designed instruments, operating rooms,
and methods of anesthesia suitable for the smallest of patients. He personally
trained a generation of pediatric surgeons—most of whom are now the leaders
and teachers of this specialty—and he established divisions of pediatric surgery
for all surgical specialties at the Children's Hospital of Philadelphia.

Among the many technical developments that have benefited medicine and
surgery in general, a few are of particular help to pediatric surgery. Microsurgical techniques allow greater visibility when working with small structures;
small-sized fiberoptic endoscopes aid diagnosis, and ultrasonography enables the
diagnosis of some congenital abnormalities early in fetal life. Also, several

methods of oxygenating a baby's blood outside the body while surgery is taking place are currently in use.

Neonatal surgery focuses on the early correction of a variety of congenital abnormalities that may interfere with the vital functions of organ systems; hernias, bile ducts that are too narrow, an esophagus that is too short or too narrow, a return without an external opening, or kidneys that are so large that they may compress the lungs are but a few of the conditions that can be treated. Such congenital problems often are not entirely solved by a single procedure, but more and more patients live to benefit from subsequent operations. In spite of the intricacies of operating on very small structures in patients who are not the best risks, infants tolerate surgery surprisingly well.

Apart from congenital problems that create literally life-or-death situations, there are other cases that may require less immediate surgery; hearing defects, organ transplants, genital imperfections, and limb deformities are examples. Improved methods of replacing blood loss have made it possible to conserve organs and tissues that formerly had to be sacrificed. The spleen is an example: Four different operations have been devised to save the spleen or a part of it, with the successful result of such an operation being that the child is not deprived of the spleen's contribution to immunity.

Fetal surgery—operations on the unborn child—is now beyond the purely experimental stage. This work has been pioneered by Dr. Michael R. Harrison of the Children's Hospital of San Francisco. With ultrasonography, a graphic picture can be obtained of the unborn child, and some congenital abnormalities can now be diagnosed as early as the twelfth week of fetal life. The number of moral and ethical questions associated with this type of surgery is fully recognized by the physicians engaged in it, and they have established very strict indications. There must, of course, be minimal risk to the mother, and she must be thoroughly counseled. Operations are limited to conditions that can reasonably be expected to be less severe if operated upon before rather than after birth. At the present time, such operations are limited to three or four well-recognized conditions.

California
Children's Hospital of Los Angeles
4650 Sunset Boulevard
Los Angeles, CA 90027
(213) 660-2450
Program Director: Eric W. Fonkalsrud
(Special interest: pediatric kidney transplants)

Children's Hospital of San Francisco
3700 California Street
San Francisco, CA 94119
(415) 387-8700
Program Director: Dr. Michael Harrison
(Special interest: fetal surgery)

District of Columbia	Children's Hospital National Medical Center 111 Michigan Avenue, N. W. Washington, DC 20010 (202) 745-5000 Program Director: Dr. Judson Randolph
Illinois	Children's Memorial Hospital 2300 Children's Plaza Chicago, IL 60614 (312) 880-4338 Program Director: Dr. John G. Raffensperger
Maryland	Johns Hopkins Hospital 600 North Wolfe Street Baltimore, MD 21205 (301) 955-5000 Program Director: Dr. J. Alex Haller, Jr.
Massachusetts	Children's Hospital 300 Longwood Avenue Boston, MA 02115 (617) 735-6000 Program Director: Dr. Raphael Levey (Special interests: pediatric urology and oncology, congenital heart surgery)
Michigan	University of Michigan Hospitals 1500 East Medical Center Drive Ann Arbor, MI 48109 (313) 936-4000 Program Director: Dr. Arnold G. Coran (Special interests: neonatal surgery, inflammatory bowel diseases, Hirschsprung's disease)
Missouri	Children's Mercy Hospital 24th Street at Gillham Road Kansas City, MO 64108 (816) 234-3000 Program Director: Dr. Raymond Armoury
New York	Children's Hospital of Buffalo 219 Bryant Street Buffalo, NY 14222 (716) 878-7000 Program Director: Dr. Donald R. Clooney (Special interests: pediatric cardiovascular neonatology, intra-abdominal injuries, orthopedic surgery)

Columbia-Presbyterian Medical Center
622 West 168th Street
New York, NY 10032
(212) 305-2500
Program Director: Dr. R. Peter Altman

Ohio

Children's Hospital Medical Center
Elland and Bethesda Avenues
Cincinnati, OH 45229
(513) 559-4200
Program Director: Dr. Lester Martin
(Special interests: ulcerative colitis, Hirschsprung's
    disease)

Children's Hospital
700 Children's Drive
Columbus, OH 43205
(614) 461-2312
Program Director: Dr. E. Thomas Boles, Jr.
(Special interest: pediatric oncology)

Oklahoma

Oklahoma Children's Memorial Hospital
P. O. Box 26307
Oklahoma City, OK 73126
(405) 271-5911
Program Director: Dr. William Tunell

Pennsylvania

Children's Hospital of Philadelphia
34th Street at Civic Center Boulevard
Philadelphia, PA 19104
(215) 596-9100
Program Director: Dr. James O'Neill, Jr.
(Special interests: pediatric oncology and urology)

Children's Hospital of Pittsburgh
125 De Sota Street
Pittsburgh, PA 15213
(412) 692-5700
Program Director: Dr. Marc Rowe
(Special interests: liver transplants, research into
    metabolism of the newborn)

Tennessee

Vanderbilt University Medical Center
1211 22nd Avenue, South
Nashville, TN 37232
(615) 322-7311
Program Director: Dr. John Sawyers

Texas   Texas Children's Hospital
                           6621 Fannin Street
                           Houston, TX 77030
                           (713) 798-1000
                           Program Director: Dr. Charles McCollum
                           (Special interest: cardiac surgery for children)

Washington   Children's Orthopedic Hospital and Medical
                             Center
                           4800 Sand Point Way, N. E.
                           Seattle, WA 98105
                           (206) 526-2000
                           Program Director: Dr. David Tapper

PLASTIC AND RECONSTRUCTIVE SURGERY

Modern plastic surgery became firmly established during and after World War II. Two centers in England, devoted exclusively to the care of military personnel who had sustained mutilating injuries and disfigurements, treated patients in great numbers while also training surgeons from many countries. In the United States, Dr. Robert Ivy of the University of Pennsylvania was a pioneer in establishing standards of treatment and care. The development of new and safer methods of treating shock, the advent of antibiotics, and the invention of new instruments all expanded the possibilities of plastic surgery.

Congenital defects such as harelip and cleft palate are now corrected much earlier in life than was previously possible. Defects involving various parts of the body tend to be treated by specialists of those regions. The restoration of function and the improvement of cosmetic appearance are the great contributions of plastic surgery. Some of the newer facial prostheses are responsible for amazingly faithful restorations of facial features and contours disrupted by infection, cancer, or accidental injuries.

In probably no other field of medical care is it more important to seek the best. Therefore, do not take only the word of a friend or neighbor in choosing a plastic surgeon; and beware, in general, of physicians with their own private hospitals for this type of work. They should be checked out very thoroughly by you or your personal physician.

Alabama   University of Alabama
                           619 South 19th Street
                           Birmingham, AL 35294
                           (205) 934-3245
                           Program Director: Dr. Luis O. Vasconez
                           (Special interests: breast reconstruction, aesthetic sur-
                             gery, cleft lip and palate)

California	University of California San Francisco Hospitals and Clinics 505 Parnassus Avenue San Francisco, CA 94143 (415) 476-1000 Program Director: Dr. Stephen J. Mathes (Special interests: breast reconstruction, microvascular reimplantation, tissue-transfer research, trauma)
	University of Southern California Medical Center 1200 North State Street Los Angeles, CA 90033 (213) 226-2345 Program Director: Dr. John F. Reinisch
	Stanford University Medical Center 300 Pasteur Drive Stanford, CA 94305 (415) 723-4000 Program Director: Dr. Lars Vistnes (Special interests: ophthalmic plastic surgery, surgery of the hand)
Florida	Jackson Memorial Hospital 1611 N. W. 12th Avenue Miami, FL 33136 (305) 325-7429 Program Director: Dr. D. Ralph Millard, Jr. (Special interests: cleft lip, cleft palate)
	Shands Hospital—University of Florida 1600 S. W. Archer Road Gainesville, FL 32610 (904) 392-3711 Program Director: Dr. Hal Bingham (Special interests: vascular lesions, burns)
Georgia	Emory University Hospital 1364 Clifton Road, N. E Atlanta, GA 30322 (404) 321-0111 Program Director: Dr. John Bostwick III
Illinois	Southern Illinois University School of Medicine 801 North Rutledge, P. O. Box 19230 Springfield, IL 62794 (217) 782-8869 Program Director: Dr. Elvin Zook (Special interests: hand surgery, microsurgery, burns)

Kansas	University of Kansas Medical Center 39th Street and Rainbow Boulevard Kansas City, KS 66103 (913) 588-5000 Program Director: Dr. John Hiebert
Kentucky	University of Louisville Hospital 530 South Jackson Street Louisville, KY 40202 (502) 562-3000 Program Director: Dr. Leonard Weiner (Special interest: hand surgery)
Massachusetts	Brigham and Women's Hospital 75 Francis Street Boston, MA 02115 (617) 732-5500 Program Director: Dr. Elof Eriksson Massachusetts General Hospital 32 Fruit Street Boston, MA 02114 (617) 726-2000 Program Director: Dr. James May (Special interest: hand surgery)
Minnesota	Mayo Clinic 200 S. W. First Street Rochester, MN 55905 (507) 284-2511 Program Director: Dr. Ian Jackson (Special interest: craniofacial surgery)
Missouri	Barnes Hospital One Barnes Plaza St. Louis, MO 63110 (314) 362-7388 Program Director: Dr. Paul Weeks (Special interests: craniofacial and hand surgery)
New York	Institute for Plastic and Reconstructive Surgery 550 First Avenue New York, NY 10016 (212) 340-5834 Program Director: Dr. Joseph G. McCarthy (Special interests: craniofacial and hand surgery)

North Carolina	North Carolina Memorial Hospital Manning Drive Chapel Hill, NC 27514 (919) 966-4131 Program Director: Dr. A. Griswold Bevin (Special interests: hand surgery, difficult wounds)
Pennsylvania	Hospital of the University of Pennsylvania 3400 Spruce Street Philadelphia, PA 19104 (215) 662-7090 Program Director: Dr. Linton A. Whitaker (Special interests: cleft lip, cleft palate, craniofacial surgery)
Texas	Baylor College of Medicine and Hospitals One Baylor Plaza Houston, TX 77030 (713) 798-4951 Program Director: Dr. Melvin Spira
Virginia	University of Virginia Hospital Jefferson Park Avenue Charlottesville, VA 22908 (804) 924-0211 Program Director: Dr. Milton T. Edgerton, Jr. (Special interests: craniofacial anomalies, birthmarks)
	Medical College of Virginia Hospital 401 North 12th Street Richmond, VA 23219 (804) 786-0932 Program Director: Dr. Kelman Cohen

UROLOGIC SURGERY
(see also chapter 3, "Medicine")

Scientific advances in the field of urologic surgery are not entirely surgical in the old-fashioned "cutting" sense of the word. Newest, perhaps, is a noninvasive, virtually painless method of removing kidney stones, requiring only a few hours in the hospital. Imported from West Germany, the method is called lithotripsy and the machine, a litho-tripter. It was invented by two German doctors at the Ludwig Maximillian University's Munich Klinikum Grosshadern. The patient is placed in a tub of water that transmits shock waves to the kidneys, pulverizing the stones to the consistency of sand. They are then excreted over a period of time. A local or a general anesthetic can be used to allay the patient's fears, and the procedure can be repeated if stones recur.

Ultrasound, now practiced in many medical centers, is another recently devised method for disintegrating kidney stones. It requires only a tiny ⅓-inch incision through which a probe is passed to the region of the stone. A hollow tube is then threaded over the probe for the passage of instruments. Sometimes the stone can be removed through the tube, but usually the ultrasound probe is placed in contact with the stone and shatters it. The gravel is removed through the tube by suction. Dr. Joseph Segra of the Mayo Clinic is well known for his work in this field, and at Baylor College of Medicine and Hospitals in Houston, Dr. F. Bramley Scott is engaged in similar work.

Alabama	University of Alabama Medical Center 619 South 19th Street/University Station Birmingham, AL 35294 (205) 934-1462 Program Director: Dr. Anton Bueschen
California	University of California Los Angeles Medical Center 10833 Le Conte Avenue Los Angeles, CA 90024 (213) 825-9111 Program Director: Dr. Jean B. de Kernion
	Stanford University Medical Center 300 Pasteur Drive Stanford, CA 94305 (415) 723-4000 Program Director: Dr. Thomas Stamey
Colorado	University of Colorado Health Sciences Center 4200 East Ninth Avenue Denver, CO 80262 (303) 329-3066 Program Director: Dr. E. David Crawford
Connecticut	Yale–New Haven Hospital 333 Cedar Street New Haven, CT 06510 (203) 785-4242 Program Director: Dr. Bernard Lytton
District of Columbia	George Washington University Hospital 901 23rd Street, N. W. Washington, DC 20037 (202) 994-1000 Program Director: Dr. Harry Miller, Jr.

Florida	Jackson Memorial Hospital 1611 N. W. 12th Avenue Miami, FL 33136 (305) 325-7429 Program Director: Dr. Victor Politano
	Shands Hospital—University of Florida 1600 S. W. Archer Road Gainesville, FL 32610 (904) 392-2501 Program Director: Dr. David Drylie
Georgia	Emory University Hospital 1364 Clifton Road, N. E. Atlanta, GA 30322 (404) 321-0111 Program Director: Dr. Samuel S. Ambrose
Illinois	Northwestern University Medical Center 250 East Superior Street Chicago, IL 60611 (312) 908-8145 Program Director: Dr. John Grayhack
Indiana	Methodist Hospital of Indiana 1701 North Senate Boulevard/P. O. Box 1367 Indianapolis, IN 46206 (317) 924-6411 Program Director: Dr. John Donohue
Iowa	University of Iowa Hospitals and Clinics 650 Newton Road Iowa City, IA 52242 (319) 356-2934 Program Director: Dr. Richard Williams
Louisiana	Alton Ochsner Medical Foundation 1516 Jefferson Highway New Orleans, LA 70121 (504) 838-3000 Program Director: Dr. William Brannan
	Tulane Medical Center Hospital and Clinics 1415 Tulane Avenue New Orleans, LA 70112 (504) 588-5471 Program Director: Dr. Blackwell Evans

Maryland   Johns Hopkins Hospital
                          600 North Wolfe Street
                          Baltimore, MD 21205
                          (301) 955-5000
                          Program Director: Dr. Patrick Walsh

                          University of Maryland Medical Systems
                          22 South Greene Street
                          Baltimore, MD 21201
                          (301) 328-5666
                          Program Director: Dr. Edward Campbell

Massachusetts   University Hospital
                          88 East Concord Street
                          Boston, MA 02118
                          (617) 638-8000
                          Program Director: Dr. Robert Krane

                          Massachusetts General Hospital
                          32 Fruit Street
                          Boston, MA 02114
                          (617) 726-2000
                          Program Director: Dr. George Prout, Jr.

Michigan   University of Michigan Hospitals
                          1500 East Medical Center Drive
                          Ann Arbor, MI 48109
                          (313) 936-4000
                          Program Director: Dr. Edward McGuire

                          Henry Ford Hospital
                          2799 West Grand Boulevard
                          Detroit, MI 48202
                          (313) 876-2600
                          Program Director: Dr. Joseph Cerny

Minnesota   Mayo Clinic
                          200 S. W. First Street
                          Rochester, MN 55905
                          (507) 284-2511
                          Program Director: Dr. P. P. Kelalis

New York   Buffalo General Hospital
                          100 High Street
                          Buffalo, NY 14203
                          (716) 845-5600
                          Program Director: Dr. Gerald Sufrin

New York Hospital—Cornell Medical Center
525 East 68th Street
New York, NY 10021
(212) 746-5454
Program Director: Dr. E. Daracott Vaughn, Jr.

North Carolina North Carolina Memorial Hospital
Manning Drive
Chapel Hill, NC 27514
(919) 966-4131
Program Director: Dr. Floyd Fried

Duke University Medical Center
Box 3005
Durham, NC 27710
(919) 684-5587
Program Director: Dr. David Paulson

Ohio Cleveland Clinic Foundation
9500 Euclid Avenue
Cleveland, OH 44106
(216) 444-2200
Program Director: Dr. Drogo K. Montague

Pennsylvania Temple University Hospital
3401 North Broad Street
Philadelphia, PA 19140
(215) 221-2000
Program Director: Dr. A. Richard Kendall

Tennessee University of Tennessee Medical Center
956 Court Avenue
Memphis, TN 38103
(901) 528-5868
Program Director: Dr. Clair Cox

Texas Baylor College of Medicine and Hospitals
One Baylor Plaza
Houston, TX 77030
(713) 798-4951
Program Director: Dr. Peter T. Scardino

Washington University of Washington Medical Center
1959 N. E. Pacific Street
Seattle, WA 98195
(206) 543-3640
Program Director: Dr. Paul H. Lange

VASCULAR SURGERY

Operations upon blood vessels are variously classified according to the size of the vessel, its location within the body, or its association with an organ system of the body. Operations upon particular vessels, as they extend from one region to another, become the province of specialists whose interests lie in those regions. For example, the abdominal part of the aorta would tend to come within the field of an abdominal surgeon, the branches of the carotid arteries within the skull are operated upon by the neurosurgeon, and kidney vessels are considered to belong to the field of hypertensive vascular surgery.

Use of the operating microscope has made possible the joining of vessels of very small size and the bypassing of diseased areas of blood vessels. The development in the past decade of the biograft, a type of vascular transplant for saving endangered limbs from amputation, is another important area of progress. Biografts were developed by Dr. Irving Dardik of Englewood Hospital in Englewood, New Jersey. He and his brother, Dr. Herbert Dardik, originated and perfected the use of the small flexible blood vessels in the human umbilical cord for the preservation of human limbs that might otherwise be lost. Begun in 1972 at the Laboratory of Experimental Medicine and Surgery at New York University Medical Center, the biograft method may eventually be used to prevent the paralysis and other serious effects caused by prolonged loss of blood to the brain brought on by strokes.

Not surprisingly, there are quite a number of institutions that have strong departments of both cardiothoracic and vascular surgery, because there is considerable overlap in these fields. There are, however, a number of institutions that are especially well known for their work in the vascular field.

California   University of California San Francisco Hospitals and
                   Clinics
                   505 Parnassus Avenue
                   San Francisco, CA 94143
                   (415) 476-1000
                   Program Director: Dr. Jerry Goldstone

Illinois   Northwestern University Medical Center
                   250 East Superior Street
                   Chicago, IL 60611
                   (312) 908-2714
                   Program Director: Dr. James S. Yao

                   University of Chicago Hospitals and Clinics
                   5841 South Maryland Avenue
                   Chicago, IL 60637
                   (312) 947-1000
                   Program Director: Dr. Christopher K. Zarins
                   (Special interest: upper-extremity vascular surgery)

Louisiana	Alton Ochsner Medical Foundation 1516 Jefferson Highway New Orleans, LA 70121 (504) 838-3000 Program Director: Dr. Larry H. Hollier
Massachusetts	Brigham and Women's Ho●ital 75 Francis Street Boston, MA 02115 (617) 732-5500 Program Director: Dr. John Mannick (Special interests: vascular surgery of the limbs and limb reattachment)
Michigan	University of Michigan Hospitals 1500 East Medical Center Drive Ann Arbor, MI 48109 (313) 936-4000 Program Director: Dr. James C. Stanley (Special interest: renal artery surgery)
Minnesota	Mayo Clinic 200 S. W. First Street Rochester, MN 55905 (507) 284-2511 Program Director: Dr. Peter C. Pairolero
New York	New York University Medical Center First Avenue and 27th Street New York, NY 10016 (212) 340-5505 Program Director: Dr. Anthony Imparato
Ohio	St. Anthony's Hospital 1450 Hawthorne Avenue Columbus, OH 43203 (614) 251-3000 Program Director: Dr. Larey Carey (Special interests: vascular surgery of the limbs and limb reattachment)
Oregon	Oregon Health Sciences University Hospital 3181 West Sam Jackson Park Road Portland, OR 97201 (503) 225-8311 Program Director: Dr. John Porter (Special interest: upper-extremity vascular surgery)

Pennsylvania   Hospital of the University of Pennsylvania
                      3400 Spruce Street
                      Philadelphia, PA 19104
                      (215) 662-2050
                      Program Director: Dr. Clyde F. Barker

Tennessee   Vanderbilt University Medical Center
                      1211 22nd Avenue South
                      Nashville, TN 37232
                      (615) 322-7311
                      Program Director: Dr. John Sawyers
                      (Special interest: renal-artery surgery)

Texas   Baylor College of Medicine and Hospitals
                      One Baylor Place
                      Houston, TX 77030
                      (713) 798-4951
                      Program Director: Dr. E. Stanley Crawford

                      Baylor University Medical Center
                      3500 Gaston Avenue
                      Dallas, TX 75246
                      (214) 820-0111
                      Program Director: Dr. C. M. Mack Talkington

Washington   University of Washington Medical Center
                      1959 N. E. Pacific Street
                      Seattle, WA 98195
                      (206) 548-3300
                      Program Director: Dr. D. E. Strandness

· 5 ·

TRANSPLANTS: AN ERA
OF DISCOVERY

There is scarcely a more vivid picture of medical progress during the past quarter century than that which characterizes organ transplant surgery. From its beginnings in the uncertainties of research and experiment, it has moved with great assurance into the present era of therapeutic application and increasingly predictable long-term beneficial results for thousands of patients.

The dream of replacing diseased, worn-out organs with healthy donated ones has become a reality in the cases of kidney, heart, liver, pancreas, and even lung and heart-lung combinations. Among the main factors responsible for progress in this field are the advances made in typing and matching donor and recipient tissues for compatibility; the ability to neutralize certain rejection responses by means of pretransplant treatment of the donor and the recipient (in the case of live donors); improved methods of organ retrieval and storage procedures according to standardized protocols; and, most important, the use of the immunosuppressive drug cyclosporin. Used carefully—for it does have some untoward effects—cyclosporin has greatly diminished the rate of graft rejection and has lengthened the organ survival time in almost all types of transplants, particularly when used in combination with other immunosuppressive drugs.

Although certain problems in the area of organ rejection remain to be solved, the number one problem today is the lack of a sufficient number of organs to meet the growing demand. For example, about three times as many kidneys are needed by patients than are available, and all but approximately 10 percent of patients in need of a new liver die while waiting for one.

The National Organ Transplantation Act of 1984 is the culmination of several prior legislative attempts to deal with the problem of availability on a nationwide basis. It provides federal grants to qualified regional Organ Procurement Organizations (OPOs) to increase the availability of transplantable organs. It also established an Organ Procurement and Transportation Network for the computerized matching of available organs with potential recipients. Such computer programming of the possible sources of organs and the locations of need, matched for time and distance, is essential. If there is a match, the network will transport the organ to the appropriate location. The act also set up a Task Force on Organ Transplantation to report upon the medical, ethical, legal, and economic issues related to organ transplants and calls for the establishment of a scientific registry to monitor the effectiveness of this surgery and the clinical status of transplant patients. Significantly, the act *prohibits* the purchase of human organs for transplant purposes under penalty of fines and imprisonment.

Actually, there would be quite enough organs available to meet the demand if healthy transplantable organs could be obtained soon after death. Of course, much more would be needed in the way of permission from potential donors and their heirs. Transportation of dying patients to areas where their organs may be needed after they die is a possible alternative to having many usable organs buried. All it takes is an enlightened, caring population to match the strides in scientific medicine that are taking place.

KIDNEY TRANSPLANTS

The kidney was the first organ to be transplanted successfully in a human being, at the Peter Bent Brigham Hospital in Boston in the mid-1950s. Today the kidney is the most frequently transplanted organ, and kidney transplantation has the highest rate of success. Up to the beginning of 1989, approximately 87,000 kidney transplants have been performed among 218 centers capable of handling such transplants. The success rate is about 95 percent for kidneys donated by relatives of the recipient and about 90 percent for random cadaver transplants with the use of immunosuppressive drugs. (These figures are for survival rates of at least two years.)

Economically, kidney transplants are vastly preferable to dialysis (the chemical removal of wastes by machine) in patients with nonfunctioning kidneys. It is estimated that the cost of 10,000 kidney transplants compared with the cost of keeping the same number of patients on dialysis for a four-year period would produce a total savings of $400 million. The current imbalance of supply of and demand for organs to be transplanted restricts the number of patients who can return to normal or near-normal lives. The National Organ Transplantation Act is a major step toward correcting this situation.

Although almost all major medical centers have facilities for the transplant of kidneys, those listed here are among the very best in this field.

Alabama   University of Alabama Medical Center
                   619 South 19th Street/University Station
                   Birmingham, AL 35294
                   (205) 934-4011

California	Stanford University Hospital 300 Pasteur Drive Stanford, CA 94305 (415) 723-4000
Florida	Jackson Memorial Hospital 1611 N. W. 12th Avenue Miami, FL 33136 (305) 325-7429 Program Director: Dr. Joshua Miller
Maryland	Johns Hopkins Hospital 600 North Wolfe Street Baltimore, MD 21205 (301) 955-5000
Massachusetts	Brigham and Women's Hospital 75 Francis Street Boston, MA 02115 (617) 732–5500
New York	Columbia-Presbyterian Medical Center 622 West 168th Street New York, NY 10032 (212) 305-2500
Pennsylvania	University Health Center of Pittsburgh 121 Meyran Avenue Pittsburgh, PA 15260 (412) 647-2345
Tennessee	Vanderbilt University Medical Center 1211 22nd Avenue, South Nashville, TN 37232 (615) 322-7311

HEART TRANSPLANTS

It is estimated that in the 23 years since the first heart transplant surgery, under the direction of Dr. Norman Shumway of Stanford University, about 11,000 heart transplant operations have been done (up to November 1989) throughout the world, and 65 percent of these have been done in U.S. medical centers. The number of centers offering this service has increased from 2 in 1976 to 148 in 1989. According to statistics compiled by the International Society for Heart Transplantation, patient survival rates worldwide, for one, two, and five years are 80, 77, and 75 percent, respectively. Formerly as low as 20 percent at the one-year mark, the rates have been dramatically improved by newer methods of detecting tissue rejection and with the use of combinations of certain drugs that retard or prevent tissue rejection: cyclosporin, Imuran, Prednisone, and O-KT3, derived from monoclonal antibodies. Although these statistics (especially the five-year survival rates) must be viewed with the usual amount of caution, they are nevertheless impressive when we consider the fact that patients waiting for donors' hearts that are not available would have a life expectancy of a few months or less.

There is a distinct advantage in choosing a center with long experience in performing heart transplant surgery, although some very good work is being done by those institutions new to the field.

The following are heart transplant centers with long experience and strong track records.

Stanford University Medical Center
300 Pasteur Drive
Stanford, CA 94305
(415) 723-4000
Program established: 1968

Medical College of Virginia Hospital
401 North 12th Street
Richmond, VA 23219
(804) 786-0932
Program established: 1968

Columbia-Presbyterian Medical Center
622 West 168th Street
New York, NY 10032
(212) 305-2500
Program established: 1977

University of Minnesota Hospitals and Clinics
Harvard Street at East River Road
Minneapolis, MN 55455
(612) 626-3000
Program established: 1978

University of Arizona Health Sciences Center
1501 North Campbell Avenue
Tucson, AZ 85724
(602) 626-0111
Program established: 1979

St. Louis University Hospitals
1325 South Grand Boulevard
St. Louis, MO 63104
(314) 771-7600
Program established:1979

Presbyterian University Hospital
De Sota and O'Hara Streets
Pittsburgh, PA 15213
(412) 647-2345
Program established: 1980

University of Alabama Medical Center
619 South 19th Street/University Station
Birmingham, AL 35294
(205) 934-4011
Program established: 1981

Texas Heart Institute
6720 Bertner Drive
Houston, TX 77030
(713) 791-4011
Program established: 1982

Methodist Hospital of Indiana
1701 North Senate Boulevard/P. O. Box 1367
Indianapolis, IN 46206
(317) 929-2000
Program established: 1982

Johns Hopkins Hospital
600 North Wolfe Street
Baltimore, MD 21205
(301) 955-5000
Program established: 1983

Brigham and Women's Hospital
75 Francis Street
Boston, MA 02115
(617) 732-5500
Program established: 1984

Baylor College of Medicine and Hospitals
One Baylor Plaza
Houston, TX 77030
(713) 798-4951
Program established: 1984

Loyola University Medical Center
2160 South First Avenue
Maywood, IL 60153
(312) 531-3000
Program established: 1984

HEART-LUNG TRANSPLANTS

Since 1981, about 600 heart-lung transplants have been done throughout the world. Of those, about 45 percent were performed in the United States, with the largest number (71) at Stanford University (figures to November 1989).

According to the International Society for Heart Transplantation, the worldwide patient survival figures for one, two, and five years are 62, 59, and 56 percent, respectively.

LIVER TRANSPLANTS

Up to the beginning of 1989, about 3,500 liver transplants have been done in the United States. The number of medical centers with liver transplant capability has increased from 15 in 1984 to 73 in 1989. The largest number has been performed at the University of Pittsburgh Medical Center by a team under the direction of Dr. Thomas Starzl, who pioneered liver transplant surgery at the University of Colorado.

Cyclosporin and other immunosuppressive drugs have contributed to present survival rates of about 80 percent for one year and 60 percent for five years.

Transplantation of the liver is the most technically difficult of all organ transplants. It is reasonable, therefore, to recommend for this procedure centers with long experience and well-trained teams. The most highly recommended centers for this surgery are the University Health Center of Pittsburgh and the University of Minnesota Hospitals and Clinics, both included in the following list of 20 medical centers of outstanding capability in this field.

Alabama   University of Alabama Medical Center
                 619 South 19th Street/University Station
                 Birmingham, AL 35294
                 (205) 934-4011

Arizona   Good Samaritan Medical Center
                 1111 East McDowell Road
                 Phoenix, AZ 85062
                 (602) 239-2000

California   University of California Los Angeles Medical Center
                 10833 Le Conte Avenue
                 Los Angeles, CA 90024
                 (213) 825-9111

                 University of California Davis Medical Center
                 2315 Stockton Boulevard
                 Sacramento, CA 95817
                 (916) 453-3096

University of California San Diego Medical Center
225 Dickinson Street
San Diego, CA 92103
(619) 294-6222

Connecticut   Yale–New Haven Hospital
333 Cedar Street
New Haven, CT 06510
(203) 785-4242

Kansas   University of Kansas Medical Center
39th Street and Rainbow Boulevard
Kansas City, KS 66103
(913) 588-5000

Massachusetts   Children's Hospital
300 Longwood Avenue
Boston, MA 02115
(617) 735-6000

Massachusetts General Hospital
32 Fruit Street
Boston, MA 02114
(617) 726-2000

New England Deaconess Hospital
185 Pilgrim Road
Boston, MA 02115
(617) 732-7000

Tufts–New England Medical Center
171 Harrison Avenue
Boston, MA 02111
(617) 956-5000

Minnesota   University of Minnesota Hospitals
Harvard Street at East River Road
Minneapolis, MN 55455
(612) 626-3000

Mississippi   University Hospital
2500 North State Street
Jackson, MS 39216
(601) 987-4811

North Carolina   Duke University Medical Center
Box 3005
Durham, NC 27710
(919) 684-5587

Pennsylvania

Hospital of the University of Pennsylvania
3400 Spruce Street
Philadelphia, PA 19104
(215) 662-4000

Thomas Jefferson University Hospital
11th and Walnut Streets
Philadelphia, PA 19107
(215) 928-6000

University Health Center of Pittsburgh
121 Meyran Avenue
Pittsburgh, PA 15260
(412) 692-5700

Tennessee

University of Tennessee Medical Center
956 Court Avenue
Memphis, TN 38103
(901) 577-4000

Wisconsin

University of Wisconsin Hospital and Clinics
600 Highland Avenue
Madison, WI 53792
(608) 263-6400

Medical College of Wisconsin
8700 West Wisconsin Avenue
Milwaukee, WI 53226
(414) 778-4040

PANCREAS TRANSPLANTS

Although progress continues in the transplant surgery of this organ, the clinical role of pancreas transplants is not so firmly established as that for, say, heart or liver transplants. In more than 75 percent of transplants of this organ, it is combined with kidney transplant. The world's leading center for this type of transplant surgery is the University of Minnesota Hospitals and Clinics in Minneapolis, where more than 300 transplants have been performed in the past ten years. In 1988, 58 transplants of the pancreas were done there, of which 51 were combined with kidney transplant.

Transplantation of only the insulin-producing cells, islets of Langerhans, is favored by some centers. Among the nonsurgical advances in the treatment of pancreatic diabetes are an infusion pump to regulate insulin dosage and synthetically produced insulin.

Minnesota

University of Minnesota Hospitals
Harvard Street at East River Road
Minneapolis, MN 55455
(612) 626-3000

BONE-MARROW TRANSPLANTS

Unlike other lifesaving donor operations, the bone-marrow transplant, used to combat certain types of leukemia, is not dangerous to the living donor—usually a brother or sister (preferably of the same sex as the recipient) whose bone marrow is a close genetic match. From the center of the body's larger bones (the breast-, upper thigh-, and hipbones) the donor's marrow is withdrawn with a large-bore needle. According to Dr. E. M. Bortin, hematologist of the International Bone Marrow Transplant Registry and a member of the bone-marrow transplant team at the Fred Hutchinson Cancer Research Center in Seattle, the instance of any resulting donor complications is a tiny fraction of 1 percent, and there are no permanent aftereffects.

For the recipient, who is already dying of leukemia, it can be quite another matter. Half of all bone-marrow recipients ("hosts" to the matched marrow) develop a genetic problem termed "graft-versus-host" (GVH), with about a 50 percent survival rate from this and other complications. Most cancer care centers in the United States are equipped to perform bone-marrow transplants, and each year more hospitals are adding bone-marrow units. (See chapter 6, "Cancer: Meeting the Challenge," for a more extensive list of cancer centers.) Some especially recommended centers for bone-marrow transplants are:

California   University of California Los Angeles Medical Center
                      10833 Le Conte Avenue
                      Los Angeles, CA 90024
                      (213) 825-9111

Minnesota   Methodist Hospital
                      201 West Center Street
                      Rochester, MN 55905
                      (507) 286-7890

North Carolina   Duke University Medical Center
                      Box 3005
                      Durham, NC 27710
                      (919) 684-5587

Washington   University of Washington Medical Center
                      1959 N. E. Pacific Street
                      Seattle, WA 98195
                      (206) 548-3300

· 6 ·
CANCER: MEETING
THE CHALLENGE

Oncology is the science of tumors, which are abnormal growths of cells anywhere in the body. The great majority of tumors are benign, tend not to recur after surgical removal, and are not life-threatening. Their size may vary from that of a small skin mole to that of a goiter larger than a football. Some benign tumors may undergo malignant change; others are malignant only in the sense that they encroach upon vital structures.

Cancer is the general word used to indicate malignancy. There are more than 100 kinds of malignant tumors. Also considered with these malignancies are the leukemias—diseases involving abnormalities of the white blood cells. Unless diagnosed early, malignant tumors generally tend toward uncontrolled growth, crowding out normal cells. They may spread locally or become seeded, via the bloodstream, in various remote parts of the body. Early diagnosis offers the best chance for successful treatment. Although the death rate began to decline in 1984 for the first time, mainly owing to an increased awareness on the part of the public of the early symptoms and signs rather than to advances in treatment.

"If only we could find the causes" is the plea of all humanity. The good news is that some of the most essential experimental work for finding the causes of cancer is nearing completion. The past few years have recorded some fantastic breakthroughs in understanding the biology of malignant cells. It seems doubtful, however, that one single cause of all malignant tumors will be found. Individuals apparently differ in their abilities to resist the transformation from normal to abnormal cells. For some people, even a lowered state of resistance may be enough to protect the body if it is not overwhelmed by environmental factors.

The role of diet as a possible cancer preventive is the subject of much research. Its importance, in at least one type of cancer, is illustrated by the higher incidence of stomach cancer among certain groups of Japanese and Icelanders whose diets include much smoked fish. A diet overbalanced with meat and short on roughage is thought to have some bearing on intestinal cancer. In this connection, Dr. Peter Greenwald, director of the National Cancer Institute's Division of Cancer Control and Prevention, offers this advice: Eat foods high in fiber content, low in fat (which has been linked to some types of cancer), and take vitamins C, E, and A along with the mineral silenium. Three or four servings of fresh fruit and vegetables each day is also recommended. The NCI also warns people to avoid tobacco, unnecessary X rays, and too much sunlight.

The influence of heredity is far from clear, but more answers are expected as genetic engineering research, applied to the study of cancer, progresses. It is known, for example, that a tumor in the breast of a woman whose mother and sister have been diagnosed as having breast cancer is more apt to be cancerous than it would be without such a family history.

Cancer research is of two main types: (1) application of the basic sciences to the study of cell structure and function and (2) clinical investigation of patients with tumors and their responses to various methods of treatment.

Research in cell biology begins by asking questions about how normal cells become transformed into abnormal ones. A given experiment may not answer the questions asked, but it may suggest better questions. Among scientists of similar education are a few gifted ones who are more perceptive than the rest. Such a scientist is Dr. Barbara McClintock, the 1983 Nobel Laureate in medicine. She observed 40 years ago what presumably was there for any skilled cytologist to see—the transposition of genes in cells of corn. This phenomenon is now being observed in human tumor cells. Another promising line of research involves the use of antibodies. Vast quantities of antibodies cloned in the laboratory can interact with the known antigens of some tumors, and through this process, a vaccine for some types of cancer may be on the horizon.

The immediate concern of clinical research is the survival of patients who have cancer. Doctors have found that by employing combinations of techniques, amputation can now be avoided in certain bone cancers of the arms and legs. A study by Dr. Steven Rosenberg of the National Cancer Institute demonstrated, for example, that for certain kinds of limb tumors a limited degree of surgery, when followed by drugs and radiation, halted the spread of the tumor— something that could only be done previously through amputation.

In the past, there has been considerable fragmentation of effort among different groups doing research on the same problem. There was lack of uniformity in diagnosis, in programming clinical trials, and in analyzing results. This situation is now markedly improved, owing mainly to the efforts of a number of private and public health agencies. Among these organizations are the Cancer Commission of the American College of Surgeons, the American Joint Commission on Cancer, the National Cancer Institute, and the American Cancer Society. Such factors as the grading of tumors according to degree of malignancy, prospective studies in which diagnostic and other data are compared *before* patients are assigned to treatment programs, and standards for tumor registries designed for long-term follow-up on the progress of patients are directly translatable into improved treatment methods and the survival of more patients.

THE DETECTION OF CANCER

Nothing about cancer is more important than the awareness of its various signs and symptoms. These signs include: (1) any painless lump that can be seen or felt; (2) a headache that does not respond to usual treatment; (3) visual disturbances; (4) hearing loss, ear noises, and dizziness; (5) a cough that persists; (6) hoarseness that persists; (7) sores anywhere in the body that recur or do not heal; (8) unexplained swelling anywhere in the body; (9) changes in appetite, weight, and bowel habits; (10) abnormal or persistent bleeding or other discharges from any of the body openings; (11) unusual fatigue; (12) unexplained pain of any type.

The first step in determining whether these signs may be due to cancer is a complete physical examination. Basic laboratory tests of the blood chemistry, urine, and sometimes on the spinal fluid are helpful. If a tumor is located on the skin or just inside a body opening, it may easily be discovered. Examination of cells taken from mucous membrane areas sometimes provides important clues; this is the basis of the Pap smear for the detection of cervical cancer. Tumors farther within the body can be visualized with the help of special tubular instruments that carry light. The fiberoptics technique allows light to be bent around corners through flexible tubes. All but a small portion of the gastrointestinal tract, for example, can now be visualized by this method.

Although endoscopic methods are useful for the diagnosis of small lesions that are either confined to or penetrate into surface areas, they are not a substitute for careful X-ray examinations. A tumor must attain some size before it casts a shadow on an X-ray film. Refinements of X-ray techniques, however, are permitting smaller and smaller tumors to be diagnosed. Computerized axial tomography (CAT) scanning now allows three-dimensional images to be constructed for most areas of the body.

Magnetic resonance imaging (MRI), a noninvasive scanning technique, is a distinct contribution to the more precise diagnosis of the location and extent of tumors. Many medical centers, in addition to the 25 "best" listed in chapter 2, now have this diagnostic capability. MRI does not involve the use of X rays; instead, the area of the body to be studied is wrapped in a magnetic field. By means of radio waves, a scanner measures the effect of the magnetic field upon certain metals within the nuclei of tissue cells. Computerized pictures not only show alterations of body structure but also may indicate biochemical and metabolic factors characteristic of certain types of tumors.

Notwithstanding the great improvements in all methods of diagnostic study, the examination of a piece of the tumor under a microscope is still the most important. This is called a biopsy. After the area of the tumor has been localized, a large-bore needle is used to remove a sample of the tumor. Depending upon its location, surgical excision of the sample may be necessary. Cells within the same tumor may differ in their degrees of malignancy; therefore examination of more than just one part of a tumor is safest.

TREATMENT OF CANCER

Decisions about the treatment program for any malignant tumor depend upon a number of factors, including its kind, location, extent, and degree of malignancy. These decisions are arrived at through the collective input of medical and surgical oncologists, radiologists, chemotherapists, pathologists, and others. The National Cancer Institute has greatly improved the rapid transfer of vital medical information to doctors at hospitals in the United States with its computerized data service known as PDQ. Currently available at several thousand medical school and hospital libraries, the service describes the latest, most accepted way to treat tumors and also provides lists of cancer specialists on a regional basis.

Although cooperation is becoming more the rule, there is still too much competition for the control of the cancer patient among the different specialties. Patients are often confused as to who should be in charge—it should be a medical oncologist.

Malignant tumors are treated mainly by three methods: surgery, radiation, and chemotherapy. Another method recently developed, is immunotherapy. Each of the methods may be used alone, but more often they are used in combination or sequence depending upon the type of tumor and the patient's response at various stages of the disease. The goal of all methods is the same: to remove or kill the tumor cells while doing the least amount of harm to normal tissues. Even when tumors cannot be entirely banished by known methods of treatment, patients' lives may often be prolonged and made more comfortable.

Surgery   Statistics are variable and approximate, but it is probable that 8 million new cases of cancer will be diagnosed in the United States this year, and about 45 percent will be cured. Of the number cured, about 65 percent will be through surgery alone. The rest will be cured by a combination of surgery and one or more of the other methods of treatment.

Although advances in radiology, chemotherapy, and immunology, taken together, have supplanted the need for surgery in some cases, more radical surgery, when necessary, has been made possible and safer by a number of technical advances. These include advances in anesthetic techniques, new antibiotics to control infection, and new microsurgical instruments. Thus, it is increasingly possible for the surgeon to reconstruct, cosmetically and functionally, tissues that formerly had to be sacrificed in cancer operations.

Surgical treatment is most effective when tumors are small and localized, but it is still quite effective in many cases where there has been some spreading via the lymph nodes; it is even sometimes effective when the cancer has spread to remote areas of the body. Even when malignant tumors cannot be controlled by any methods of treatment, surgery may promote relief of discomfort in various ways.

Radiation Treatment   Radiation is the delivery of high-energy, short waves to a tumor. It is the second most common method of treating malignant tumors. External radiation is delivered from a source outside the body by X-ray or cobalt machines, or by linear accelerators. Internal radiation is achieved by the placement of various radioactive substances, such as radium, at the tumor site or by the circulation of radioactive elements through the bloodstream.

When it has been decided that radiation is needed, the radiologist will study all the available information about the patient and the tumor. More laboratory and X-ray diagnostic studies may be required to determine as accurately as possible the limits of the tumor and the areas to which it may have spread. The kind and amount of radiation is then prescribed on an individual basis. The dosage is measured in units called rads (radiation absorbed dosage). Tumors vary in the dose required for effective treatment, and patients vary in the amounts they can tolerate. At times oxygen is used to make tumors more sensitive to radiation. Computerized scans make it possible to target the rays more accurately and to minimize the exposure of normal tissues to the harmful effects of the rays. The dosage may be altered during the course of treatment depending upon the tumor's response and the patient's tolerance. The effectiveness of radiation must be balanced with the possible benefits of other methods of treatment. Radiation may reduce some tumors, otherwise inoperable, to the point where they can be surgically removed.

About one-half of all patients with malignant tumors receive radiation at some stage of their disease. When it is not effective, alone or with other treatment methods, in achieving cure or regression of the disease, it is often of great help in relieving pain and other sources of discomfort, such as bleeding and ulceration.

Chemotherapy   Chemotherapy is often used in addition to one or more of the other methods of treatment for malignant diseases. Introduction of new drugs, combinations of drugs, and the better regulation of dosages are among the factors that are expected to enlarge its contribution to treatment. At present, many doctors feel that it is overused in cases that have failed to respond to other methods of treatment. This said, it must immediately be pointed out that for perhaps a dozen kinds of tumors, chemotherapy (alone or with surgery and/or radiation) has been spectacularly successful. In certain lymphoma-type tumors, leukemias, sarcomas of soft tissue and bone, and some testicular tumors, the remission rate is astonishingly high, whereas a few years ago these same tumors were almost always fatal. Unfortunately, these are but a few of the many types of malignant tumors. The bright side of the picture is that the lower death rates from cancer of people under age 45 (and particularly under age 30) are primarily accounted for by the successful use of chemotherapy.

There are presently over 50 chemotherapeutic agents for cancer treatment. Some, such as the nitrogen mustards, are as effective today as when they were first discovered. Adriamycin, an antibiotic discovered by the Italians, is effective for some malignant diseases. Other groups of drugs, called antimetabolites, work by interfering with the energy production of cells, causing them to weaken and die. Certain hormones (adrenal gland extracts, male and female hormones) are grouped with the chemotherapeutic drugs; they are useful in the treatment of some tumors, but the ways in which they influence tumor growth are not well known.

There are, of course, some drawbacks to the use of chemotherapeutic drugs. They may harm normal cells as well as tumor-bearing ones; they may suppress the immune mechanisms that protect against infections; and, in some instances, while suppressing one type of tumor, they may encourage the growth of others. As with other kinds of treatment, there are times of hope alternating with despair.

General understanding of the usefulness of adjuvant chemotherapy and of tamoxifen, an antiestrogenic, in *early* breast cancer has been greatly enhanced by the results of a 1988 overview of 61 randomized trials among 28,896 women throughout the world. Jointly prepared by a team of British and American investigators, the report concludes: (1) cytotoxic drugs (in the most commonly used combinations) reduce the five-year mortality rate by about 25 percent in women under age 50; (2) tamoxifen reduces the five-year mortality rate by about 20 percent in women over age 50. Similar future studies may indicate which dosage forms and intervals of administration are the most beneficial, as well as long-term survival rates.

Immunology   Radiation is closely allied with the newest—and perhaps most promising—area of tumor treatment: immunology. Antibodies can be cloned and used to identify many tumor antigens. Further, these antibodies can be tagged with radioactive material for imaging tumors by radionuclide scanning. This technique has been used to treat a limited number of tumors with some success. There are also implications for improved diagnosis by means of radioactively tagged antibodies that interact with tumor antigens. Other aspects of immunological treatment involve the use of agents that stimulate the body's own immune system to kill cancer cells.

Laser Treatment   The laser beam, which converts light into thermal energy, is useful chiefly for small, localized tumors in various parts of the body such as the larynx, the bronchi, and the head and neck areas. A more reliable method of localizing some tumors and treating them involves an injection into the tumor of a blood pigment (hematoporphyrin) that is derived from hemoglobin. This sensitizes the tumor to the effects of light and the tumor is then exposed to the laser beam.

Supportive Treatment   How patients feel about themselves and their disease may be as important in cancer patients as it has been shown to be in patients who have suffered heart attacks. Dr. Jimmie Holland, chief of psychiatry at New York's Memorial Sloan-Kettering Cancer Center, heads the first comprehensive psychiatric program for cancer patients. Dr. Holland says that no matter how well he or she responds to treatment, fear of recurrence is the cancer patient's biggest problem. Thus, hospitals in many parts of the country are adding psychiatrists or psychologists to their cancer treatment teams—to provide services ranging from individual crisis intervention to relaxation with behavioral therapy.

TREATMENT CENTERS

Where to go for treatment does make a difference. The Cancer Commission of the American College of Surgeons has published a study of five-year survival rates for patients with a dozen kinds of cancer treated in various medical centers in 15 different geographic areas of the United States. For some types of cancer, survival rates differed by as much as 25 percent among centers. After allowing for variations in the methods of various programs, it was concluded that quite a few of the differences were probably owing to variations in the skill of treatment.

Although there are numerous teaching institutions with strong departments in oncology, some have reputations based mainly upon their work in particular types of cancer or upon their expertise in one form of treatment. Others emphasize clinical treatment to the exclusion of research facilities. The National Cancer Institute has funded, at considerable cost, a number of community institutions throughout the country in an effort to bring the latest cancer treatment to more people in their own communities. Some of these local hospitals and clinics are loosely affiliated with teaching institutions; others have no such connection. The treatment of cancer is multidisciplinary, and the *best* results demand the presence of skilled pathologists, cytologists, immunologists, and biochemists as well as surgeons, radiologists, and chemotherapists.

Following is a list of institutions of outstanding reputation for the diagnosis and treatment of patients with a wide variety of tumor-related diseases. Marked with an asterisk (*) are those that have been designated as comprehensive cancer centers by the Division of Cancer Prevention and Control of the National Cancer Institute. This means that they are involved in basic research as well as clinical diagnosis, clinical research, and treatment. Those marked with two asterisks (**) are involved in clinical research and treatment only.

Alabama   * University of Alabama Comprehensive Cancer
                                 Center
                             1918 University Boulevard
                             Basic Health Sciences Building, Room 108
                             Birmingham, AL 35294
                             (205) 934-6612
                             Program Director: Dr. Albert LoBuglio

Arizona

* University of Arizona Cancer Center
1501 North Campbell Avenue
Tucson, AZ 85724
(602) 626-6372
Program Director: Dr. Sydney Salmon

California

* University of Southern California Comprehensive
   Cancer Center
Kenneth Norris Jr. Cancer Hospital and Research
   Institute
1441 Eastlake Avenue
Los Angeles, CA 90033-0804
(213) 226-2370
Program Director: Dr. Brian Henderson

* Jonsson Comprehensive Cancer Center (UCLA)
10-247 Factor Building
10833 Le Conte Avenue
Los Angeles, CA 90024-1781
(213) 825-8727
Program Director: Dr. Richard Steckel

** City of Hope National Medical Center
Beckman Research Institute
1500 East Duarte Road
Duarte, CA 91010
(818) 359-8111, ext. 2292
Program Director: Dr. Charles Mittman

** University of California at San Diego Cancer
    Center
225 Dickinson Street
San Diego, CA 92103
(619) 534-6178
Program Director: Dr. Charles Mittman

Charles R. Drew University of Medicine and
   Science (consortium)
12714 South Avalon Boulevard, Suite 301
Los Angeles, CA 90061
(213) 603-3120
Program Director: Dr. Alfred Hanes

Northern California Cancer Center (consortium)
1301 Shoreway Road
Belmont, CA 94002
(415) 591-4484
Program Director: Dr. Thomas Davis

Colorado

** University of Colorado Cancer Center
4200 East 9th Avenue, Box B190
Denver, CO 80262
(303) 270-3019
Program Director: Dr. Paul Bunn, Jr.

Connecticut

* Yale University Comprehensive Cancer Center
33 Cedar Street
New Haven, CT 06510
(203) 785-6338
Program Director: Dr. Alan Sartorelli

District of
Columbia

* Howard University Cancer Research Center
2041 Georgia Avenue, N. W.
Washington, DC 20060
(202) 636-7610 or 636-5665
Program Director: Dr. Jack White

* Vincent T. Lombardi Cancer Research Center
Georgetown University Medical Center
3800 Reservoir Road, N. W.
Washington, DC 20007
(202) 687-2110
Program Director: Dr. John Potter

Florida

* Papanicolaou Comprehensive Cancer Center
University of Miami Medical School
1475 N. W. 12th Avenue
Miami, FL 33136
(305) 548-4850
Program Director: Dr. C. Gordon Zubrod

Illinois

* Illinois Cancer Council (includes institutions listed
and several other organizations)

Illinois Cancer Council
36 South Wabash Avenue
Chicago, IL 60603
(312) 226-2371
Program Director: Dr. Shirley Lansky

University of Chicago Cancer Research Center
5841 South Maryland Avenue
Chicago, IL 60637
(312) 702-6180
Program Director: Dr. John Ultmann

Kentucky   ** Lucille Parker Markey Cancer Center
                      University of Kentucky Medical Center
                      800 Rose Street
                      Lexington, KY 40536-0093
                      (606) 257-4447
                      Program Director: Dr. James Glenn

Maryland   * Johns Hopkins Oncology Center
                      600 North Wolfe Street
                      Baltimore, MD 21205
                      (301) 955-8638
                      Program Director: Dr. Albert Owens, Jr.

Massachusetts   * Dana-Farber Cancer Institute
                      44 Binney Street
                      Boston, MA 02115
                      (617) 732-3214
                      Program Director: Dr. Emil Frei III

Michigan   * Meyer L. Prentis Comprehensive Cancer Center of
                        Metropolitan Detroit
                      110 East Warren Avenue
                      Detroit, MI 48201
                      (313) 833-0710, ext. 429
                      Program Director: Dr. Michael Brennan

                      ** University of Michigan Cancer Center
                      101 Simpson Drive
                      Ann Arbor, MI 48109-0752
                      (313) 936-2516
                      Program Director: Dr. Max Wicha

Minnesota   * Mayo Comprehensive Cancer Center
                      200 S. W. First Street
                      Rochester, MN 55905
                      (507) 284-3413
                      Program Director: Dr. Charles Moertel

New Hampshire   ** Norris Cotton Cancer Center
                      Dartmouth-Hitchcock Medical Center
                      2 Maynard Street
                      Hanover, NH 03756
                      (603) 646-5485
                      Program Director: Dr. O. Ross McIntyre

New York

* Memorial Sloan-Kettering Cancer Center
1275 York Avenue
New York, NY 10021
(800) 525-2225
Program Director: Dr. Paul Marks

* Columbia University Cancer Center
College of Physicians and Surgeons
630 West 168th Street
New York, NY 10032
(212) 305-6730
Program Director: Dr. Harold Ginsberg

* Roswell Park Memorial Institute
Elm and Carlton Streets
Buffalo, NY 14263
(716) 845-4400
Program Director: Dr. Gerald Murphy

** Mt. Sinai School of Medicine
One Gustav Levy Place
New York, NY 10029
(212) 241-8617
Program Director: Dr. James Holland

** Albert Einstein College of Medicine
1300 Morris Park Avenue
Bronx, NY 10461
(212) 920-4826
Program Director: Dr. Harry Eagle

** New York University Cancer Center
462 First Avenue
New York, NY 10016-9103
(212) 340-6485
Program Director: Dr. Vittorio Defendi

** University of Rochester Cancer Center
601 Elmwood Avenue, Box 704
Rochester, NY 14642
(716) 275-4911
Program Director: Dr. Robert Couper, Jr.

North Carolina

* Duke University Comprehensive Cancer Center
P. O. Box 3843
Durham, NC 27710
(919) 684-6342 or 286-5515
Program Director: Dr. William Shingleton

** Lineberger Cancer Research Center
University of North Carolina School of Medicine
Chapel Hill, NC 27599
(919) 966-4431
Program Director: Dr. Joseph Pagano

** Bowman Gray School of Medicine
Wake Forest University
300 South Hawthorne Road
Winston-Salem, NC 27103
(919) 748-4354
Program Director: Dr. Robert Capizzi

Ohio

* Ohio State University Comprehensive Cancer
   Center
410 West 12th Avenue
Columbus, OH 43210
(614) 293-8619
Program Director: Dr. David Yohn

** Case Western Reserve University
University Hospitals of Cleveland
Ireland Cancer Center
2074 Abington Road
Cleveland, Oh 44106
(216) 844-8453

Pennsylvania

* Fox Chase Cancer Center
7701 Burholme Avenue
Philadelphia, PA 19111
(215) 728-2570
Program Director: Dr. John Durant

* University of Pennsylvania Cancer Center
3400 Spruce Street
Philadelphia, PA 19104
(215) 662-6364
Program Director: Dr. Richard Cooper

** Pittsburgh Cancer Institute
230 Lothrop Street
Pittsburgh, PA 15213-2592
(800) 537-4063
Program Director: Dr. Ronald Herberman

Rhode Island	**	Roger Williams General Hospital 825 Chalkstone Avenue Providence, RI 02908 (401) 456-2070 Program Director: Dr. Paul Calabresi
Tennessee	**	St. Jude Children's Research Hospital 332 North Lauderdale Street Memphis, TN 38101 (901) 522-0694 Program Director: Dr. Joseph Simone
Texas	*	University of Texas M. D. Anderson Cancer Center 1515 Holcombe Boulevard Houston, TX 77030 (713) 792-6161 Program Director: Dr. Charles LeMaistre
Utah	**	Utah Regional Cancer Center University of Utah Medical Center 50 North Medical Drive, Room 2C10 Salt Lake City, UT 84132 (801) 581-4048 Program Director: Dr. J. Robert Stewart
Vermont	**	Vermont Regional Cancer Center University of Vermont 1 South Prospect Street Burlington, VT 05401 (802) 656-4580 Program Director: Dr. Roger Foster, Jr.
Virginia	**	Massey Cancer Center Medical College of Virginia Virgina Commonwealth University 1200 East Broad Street Richmond, VA 23298 (804) 786-9641 Program Director: Dr. Walter Lawrence, Jr.
	**	University of Virginia Medical Center Box 334 Primary Care Center, Room 4520 Lee Street Charlottesville, VA 22908 (804) 924-2562 Program Director: Dr. Thomas O'Leary

Washington   * Fred Hutchinson Cancer Research Center
                  1124 Columbia Street
                  Seattle, WA 98104
                  (206) 467-4675
                  Program Director: Dr. Robert Day

Wisconsin   * Wisconsin Clinical Cancer Center
                  University of Wisconsin
                  600 Highland Avenue
                  Madison, WI 53792
                  (608) 263-6872
                  Program Director: Dr. Paul Carbone

For additional information about cancer, write to the Office of Cancer Communications, National Cancer Institute, Bethesda, MD 20892, or call the toll-free telephone number of the Cancer Information Service: 1-800-4-CANCER. In Hawaii, on Oahu, call 524-1234 (neighbor islands call collect). Spanish-speaking staff members are available to callers from the following areas (daytime hours only): California, Florida, Georgia, Illinois, New Jersey (area code 201), New York, and Texas.

· 7 ·

THE HEART: THE
SOURCE OF LIFE

In its healthy state, the heart works as an extremely efficient and durable pump. It is in fact a double pump, for at the same time that it receives impure blood from the body and delivers it to the lungs (the work of the right side of the heart), it receives oxygenated blood from the lungs and pumps it to the rest of the body (the work of the left side of the heart). This work is accomplished by regular contractions of the heart muscle; between contractions, it rests for a fraction of a second. Until recently, this pumping action of the heart was thought to be its only function. Recent research, still in its earliest stages, suggests that certain heart cells activate several hormones which appear to influence emotions.

The heart's efficiency as a pump is mainly determined by its output, that is, its ability to meet the body's demands for blood under the ordinary conditions of movement, exercise, sleep, and so forth. Also, the heart has certain reserves by which it can increase its output to meet the extra need in such situations as fever, weight gain, high blood pressure, and physical stress (athletes may require up to ten times the normal output during exercise). The heart does this by increasing its rate of beating, by dilating temporarily, or by enlarging permanently. When the heart's compensatory powers are used up, there is a state of comparative failure. This state may not be evident during resting conditions, but may become apparent when there are increased demands and is usually preceded by a drop in output.

The cardiologist is concerned with an individual's general state of health, particularly as it relates to heart function. Obviously, the prevention of heart disease is decidedly better than any method of treatment. Although still the leading overall cause of death in the United States (and most other countries), the incidence of heart disease is declining, particularly in the young. People are taking seriously the relationship of heart disease to high blood pressure, smoking, diet and weight, excessive consumption of alcohol, lack of regular exercise, and the many stressful conditions of modern life.

Clinical examination by the trained cardiologist is still the most important aspect of diagnosis. The skilled clinician is in the best position to evaluate the various symptoms and signs so that heart disease, if present, will not be overlooked or wrongly diagnosed. Observing the rate and quality of pulses, listening carefully to the heart sounds and the changes in these sounds occurring with a change of body position, examining the beating heart under the fluoroscope, and stress-testing on the treadmill enable the skilled cardiologist to reach an accurate diagnosis in most cases. The electrocardiogram, used by itself, is beneficial for diagnosing only a very few heart conditions, although it is helpful in confirming diagnoses and in monitoring the progress of several diseases. When indicated, special examinations such as cardiac catheterization and angiography are very useful aids to the diagnosis of some heart diseases.

Detailed classification of heart diseases, as well as the classification of disturbances of rhythm, is far beyond the scope of this volume, but most can be encapsulated under the following major headings.

Congenital heart disease, in which the defects occur early in fetal life, can be detected at birth or during the early years. Detailed study of congenital heart disease was pioneered by the late Dr. Helen B. Taussig who, with the late Dr. Alfred Blalock, devised operations to correct some defects before open-heart surgery was possible.

Infectious agents such as bacteria, viruses, and parasites still cause heart attacks, but less frequently since the advent of antimicrobial drugs.

Environmental heart diseases, caused by a lack or overabundance of minerals or other natural substances, respond well to treatment that supplies the deficient substance (such as thiamine, sodium, potassium, or thyroid hormone) or else curtails the overabundant substance.

Miscellaneous causes include injuries caused by blows to the chest, certain "allergic" vascular diseases, and tumors arising in the heart muscle. In addition to diseases that affect the heart directly, there are a number that affect it secondarily, as in certain diseases of the lungs, liver, kidneys, and thyroid gland. Sometimes the load on the heart caused by these diseases aggravates existing heart disease; control of the extracardiac disease can be expected to improve heart function.

Arteriosclerotic heart disease is, by far, the largest category of heart disease affecting older and, increasingly, middle-aged groups of the population. It involves changes occurring in the arteries such as clogging of the arteries and their loss of elasticity, both of which impede blood flow to the heart. Answers to the questions of what causes arteries to weaken is the goal of some important research, including studies of the diets of different population groups, and analyses of "life-styles" and "personality types." One interesting approach to the problem was taken in a study a number of years ago by Dr. Alexander Leaf of Harvard Medical School. He visited several parts of the world where people live to be very old; 100 years of age is not unusual in many of these societies. These groups usually live in mountainous regions where they tend sheep, thus providing regular exercise. Their diet consists of bread, milk, and cheese for the most part, but on feast days they freely indulge in all sorts of food. After long, steep mountain climbs, their heart and breathing rates change very little.

Just as the causes of arteriosclerotic heart disease are imperfectly known, so too are the reasons for the variety of its effects upon people with apparently similar degrees of the disease. There are variations in severity of symptoms, responses to treatment, and in the life span those with the disease may expect.

The heart attack takes three main forms, mainly depending on the degree of narrowing in the coronary arteries that deprives the heart muscle of needed oxygen. It may progress to a point and then stop, but usually the condition progresses from the mild to the severe form.

1. Angina pectoris is characterized by brief bouts of pain in the chest, sometimes radiating to the neck, jaw, or arms, and may occur only after strenuous effort, such as walking against a stiff wind, climbing stairs, and so on. It is usually controlled by nitroglycerin or other vessel dilators. Many of its victims live to advanced age, placing a nitroglycerin pill under the tongue when the pain occurs and never experiencing the more severe forms of attack.

2. Coronary insufficiency is characterized by more severe and longer-lasting pain. It is not always possible to distinguish it at first from coronary occlusion. Rest and anticoagulants are the main treatment.

3. Coronary occlusion is the most severe form of attack. Depending upon the artery involved, there may not be much pain, but usually there is an excruciating, viselike pain beneath the breastbone, lasting much longer than in milder attacks. There is usually shortness of breath, restlessness, profound weakness, and sometimes nausea; collapse may follow. Coronary occlusion is caused by the formation of a clot on or near fat deposits on the arterial linings. It may be a small clot or it may enlarge to completely block a large artery or one of its main branches. Occlusion of smaller branches may produce few symptoms and pass almost unnoticed—the so-called silent coronary detected only by an electrocardiogram. One of two things usually happens: either the clot may shift, allowing some blood to get through, or the blood supply to a sizable section of heart muscle may be completely shut off. The latter type is called an infarction and results in the localized "death" of muscle tissue. As with all wounds, nature then begins to clear away the debris (resulting in an elevated white-blood-cell count); in the following weeks, new blood vessels form and a scar develops around the healthy tissue. At the onset of a coronary occlusion, it is uncertain whether infarction will occur, as the signs that mark it do not appear for several days. Among these signs are changes in electrocardiogram readings, an increase in certain enzymes released into the bloodstream by dying muscle fibers, and changes in the blood count.

Cardiologists generally agree on the basic treatments of coronary occlusion: medicines to relieve pain and anxiety, administration of oxygen, management of circulatory collapse if it is present, and careful monitoring of the heart for early detection of serious disturbances of rhythm (to which a damaged heart is often prone). Treatment is best carried out in the coronary care unit (CCU) of a hospital, which has highly trained personnel and special equipment. Progress in the treatment of this condition includes the use of several materials that stop an attack while it is going on. These materials dissolve the clot and often prevent infarction of the muscle. The newest and best of these is called tissue plasmino-gen activator (t-PA), which is produced through the mass cloning of cells containing the t-PA gene. It has the advantage over similar agents of dissolving the clot where it lies—on the arterial wall—without interfering in the general factors that control bleeding and the normal clotting of blood. These clot-dissolving substances must be used within the very first hours of an attack—the earlier, the better—for they are not likely to be effective if some time has elapsed.

If the patient survives the initial shock of an occlusion (as the majority do), the most worrisome event that may then occur is an abnormal rhythm of the heartbeat, called ventricular fibrillation. This dramatically lowers the output of a heart whose circulation is already impaired. Most fatalities are associated with the inability to control this untoward event, although electric shocks to the heart may reestablish more normal rhythm and new medicines may protect against its recurrence.

Rehabilitation of the coronary patient begins in the hospital. Properly directed, rehabilitation can prevent much cardiac invalidism. In place of earlier treat-ment—enforced bed rest for a month or more after a serious heart attack—emphasis now is upon the patient's resuming some degree of activity as soon as his or her condition is stabilized, so long as such activity does not place undue strain upon the heart. Most patients can confidently expect to resume their occupations and their other activities while learning how to avoid the situations of physical and mental stress that may have contributed to their illness. Modera-tion in diet, exercise, and work habits help prevent further attacks and may reverse, to some extent, the basic arterial disease.

In these days of the undoubted overrecommendation of bypass surgery for the treatment of arteriosclerotic heart disease, it should be remembered that there have been recent advances in the medical treatment of this disease. As more and more has been learned about the pharmacology of the heart, new medicines have been introduced that help the impaired heart to do its work efficiently. These include the beta-blockers, which block the effects of adrenaline at the heart-cell level, and the calcium channel-blockers, which block the movement of harmful amounts of calcium into the heart muscle. In addition, there are improved methods of administering older cardiac drugs such as digitalis and nitroglycerin.

More time than is usual is required for the accurate prescribing of cardiac medicines. Dosages must be adjusted to fit the individual patient's requirement, not merely that of the average patient. Some drugs selected for their beneficial work on one aspect of heart disease may have adverse effects upon other aspects existing at the same time; certain drugs, when given to particular individuals, may have exactly the opposite effects of those intended. Therefore, the skilled cardiologist is in the best position not only to diagnose heart disorders but also to treat them. Too many patients are made worse by random medication at the hands of doctors who have little idea of the subtleties involved. Worse still is the frustration that can occur from inaccurate prescribing, particularly when four or five medicines are employed where one or two would do the work. This easily leads to the wrong conclusion that the patient is not being helped by medicines and therefore needs surgery. Surgery, of course, is required for the repair of congential heart defects, for the repair or replacement of damaged heart valves, for repair or grafting of major vessels leading to and from the heart, and for implanting pacemakers.

Although the number of successful heart transplant patients is increasing, comparatively few patients needing a transplant can be helped in this way because of the limited availability of suitable hearts at the right time.

Although vast sums of money are being directed toward research on the artificial heart, with limited success thus far, very few people stand to benefit by it in the immediate future. Many more heart patients would be helped by programs that have as their goal the discovery of the root causes of heart disease.

Most university-affiliated hospitals (and some that are loosely affiliated with teaching institutions) have good departments of cardiology. There are some, however, that have gained outstanding reputations through an emphasis upon numerous aspects of this specialty: research in the basic sciences as they pertain to the heart, experience in evaluating diagnostic tools and therapeutic methods; and, most important, vast clinical experience with great numbers of patients and all types of heart disease. Although a number of the institutions in the following list also have strong departments of cardiovascular surgery, their departments of cardiology exist quite independently of their surgery departments, although cooperatively, of course. Thus, patients may be quite sure of receiving studied and informed opinions as to whether or not surgery is the indicated treatment for a given condition.

One of the nation's first and most prestigious heart hospitals, the Miami Heart Institute (see Florida listing), stresses the team approach in treating both surgical and nonsurgical cases. Although it is not affiliated with a particular university, many medical professors are members of its large staff of specialists, and the institute is credited with pioneering many medical and surgical studies, such as the use of longer-lasting double mammary arteries used for coronary bypass surgery. Dr. Richard Elias, presently chairman of professional services, is one of the founders of the institute.

Alabama   University of Alabama Medical Center
                             619 South 19th Street/University Station
                             Birmingham, AL 35294
                             (205) 934-3624
                             Program Director: Dr. Gerald M. Pohost

Arizona   University of Arizona Health Sciences Center
                     1501 North Campbell Avenue
                     Tucson, AZ 85724
                     (602) 626-0111
                     Program Director: Dr. Brendan Phibbs

California   Stanford University Medical Center
                     300 Pasteur Drive
                     Stanford, CA 94305
                     (415) 723-4000
                     Acting Chief: Dr. John Schroeder

Colorado   University of Colorado Health Sciences Center
                     4200 East Ninth Avenue
                     Denver, CO 80262
                     (303) 329-3066
                     Program Director (adult cardiology): Dr. Lawrence D.
                        Horwitz
                     Program Director (pediatric cardiology): Dr. Henry
                        M. Sondheimer

Connecticut   Yale–New Haven Hospital
                     333 Cedar Street
                     New Haven, CT 06510
                     (203) 785-4242
                     Program Director (adult cardiology): Dr. Barry Zarat
                     Program Director (pediatric cardiology): Dr. Charles
                        Kleinman

Florida   Jackson Memorial Hospital
                     1611 N. W. 12th Avenue
                     Miami, FL 33136
                     (305) 549-6534
                     Program Director (adult cardiology): Dr. Robert J.
                        Myerburg
                     Program Director (pediatric cardiology): Dr. Henry
                        Gelband

                     Miami Heart Institute
                     4701 Meridian Avenue
                     Miami Beach, FL 33140
                     (305) 672-1111
                     Program Director (surgery): Dr. Martin B. Grossman
                     Program Director (cardiovascular medicine): Dr. Eu-
                        gene Saysie

Georgia

Emory University Hospital
1364 Clifton Road, N. E.
Atlanta, GA 30322
(404) 727-8147
Program Director (adult cardiology): Dr. R. Wayne
Alexander
Program Director (pediatric cardiology): Dr. Kenneth
Dooley

Illinois

Northwestern University Medical Center
250 East Superior Street
Chicago, IL 60611
(312) 908-4963
Program Director (adult cardiology): Dr. Richard
Davison
Program Director (pediatric cardiology): Dr. Wood-
row Benson, Jr.

Maryland

Johns Hopkins Hospital
600 North Wolfe Street
Baltimore, MD 21205
(301) 955-5000
Program Director (adult cardiology): Dr. Lewis C.
Becker
Program Director (pediatric cardiology): Dr. Langford
Kidd

Massachusetts

Massachusetts General Hospital
32 Fruit Street
Boston, MA 02114
(617) 726-2000
Program Director: Dr. Edgar Haber

Brigham and Women's Hospital
75 Francis Street
Boston, MA 02115
(617) 732-5500
Program Director: Dr. Thomas W. Smith

Children's Hospital
300 Longwood Avenue
Boston, MA 02115
(617) 735-6000
Program Director: Dr. Bernardo Nadal-Ginard

Minnesota	Mayo Clinic 200 S. W. First Street Rochester, MN 55905 (507) 284-2511 Program Director: Dr. Hugh C. Smith
New York	New York Hospital—Cornell Medical Center 525 East 68th Street New York, NY 01121 (212) 746-5454 Program Director (pediatric cardiology): Dr. Mary Allen Engle

North Carolina	Duke University Medical Center
	Box 3005
	Durham, NC 27710
	(919) 684-5587
	Program Director (adult cardiology): Dr. Joseph
	    Greenfield
	Program Director (pediatric cardiology): Dr. Brenda
	    Armstrong

Ohio	Cleveland Clinic Foundation 9500 Euclid Avenue Cleveland, OH 44106 (216) 444-2200 Program Director: Dr. William C. Sheldon
Pennsylvania	Hahnemann University Hospital Broad and Vine Streets Philadelphia, PA 19102 (215) 448-7000 Program Director: Dr. William S. Frankl Children's Hospital of Philadelphia 34th Street at Civic Center Boulevard Philadelphia, PA 19104 (215) 596-9100 Program Director: Dr. Henry Wagner

Tennessee	Vanderbilt University Medical Center
	1211 22nd Avenue, South
	Nashville, TN 37232
	(615) 322-7311
	Program Director (adult cardiology): Dr. Gotlieb
	    Friesinger
	Program Director (pediatric cardiology): Dr. Thomas
	    Graham, Jr.

Texas   Baylor College of Medicine and Hospitals
                       One Baylor Plaza
                       Houston, TX 77030
                       (713) 798-4951
                       Program Director (adult cardiology): Dr. Robert
                           Roberts
                       Program Director (pediatric cardiology): Dr. Arthur
                           Garson, Jr.

Virginia   University of Virginia Hospital
                       Jefferson Park Avenue
                       Charlottesville, VA 22908
                       (804) 924-0211
                       Program Director (adult cardiology): Dr. George
                           Beller
                       Program Director (pediatric cardiology): Dr. Howard
                           P. Gutgesell

Washington   University of Washington Medical Center
                       1959 N. E. Pacific Street
                       Seattle, WA 98195
                       (206) 548-3300
                       Program Director: Dr. Harold T. Dodge

· 8 ·

SOME COMMON ENEMIES

ARTHRITIS

More misconceptions about arthritis exist in the public mind than about almost any other condition of the human body. Once called "rheumatism," arthritis today refers to many painful conditions of the muscles, joints, skeletal system, and the surrounding body tissues, such as rheumatoid arthritis, bursitis, sciatica, and over one hundred other identifiable diseases. Doctors specializing in the treatment of these conditions are called rheumatologists.

According to Dr. James F. Fries, director of the Stanford University Arthritis Clinic, in his book *Arthritis,* 75 million people in the United States currently experience pain in their joints and muscles; 22 million have moderate problems from time to time; and nearly 3 million are severely affected. Arthritis, in fact, is said to cause more pain, work loss, and poor functioning than any other illness. It can be prevented, Dr. Fries maintains, with proper exercise, diet, understanding of the body's pain signals, patience, and the right treatment. Thanks to a number of technological advances such as new types of medication, surgical joint replacement when essential, and regulated physical therapy programs, medical treatment can now control all forms of this complicated disease.

Continuous research and education have solved much of the mystery surrounding what causes arthritis in men, women, and even young children, yet much remains to be discovered. The following eight categories summarized from Dr. Fries's book may help arthritis patients to better understand and identify the exact nature of their disease.

Basically, two main types of arthritis are known: (1) inflammatory, including infectious arthritis, rheumatoid arthritis and gout, all thought to be caused by autoimmune attack (other forms are called lupus erythematosus, ankylosing spondylitis, and psoriasis) and (2) noninflammatory, the most common cause of joint destruction, also called degenerative joint disease, osteoarthritis, and wear-and-tear arthritis (aging and repetitive trauma, through overuse of a joint or obesity can increase the risk of noninflammatory arthritis).

Other specific terms for arthritis are as follows:

Synovitis   In this condition, the synovial membrane surrounding a particular joint becomes inflamed, excess fluid forms, and the joint experiences painful swelling. Major synovitis is also known as rheumatoid arthritis (RA); its other forms include lupus, juvenile arthritis, and psoriatic arthritis. RA can strike anyone at any age, but is experienced mostly by women. It can be diagnosed with a simple blood test, and there can be long periods of remission. Treatment during major flare-ups is usually with pain medications and injections of cortisone, given by a skilled rheumatologist or an orthopedic surgeon familiar with individualized long-term therapy.

Attachment Arthritis   This is caused by inflammation of the ligaments attached to a bone and occurs mostly in men aged 15 to 40. It is also called ankylosing spondylitis. Treatment is most frequently with phenylbutazone.

Crystal Arthritis   This disease results from chemical crystals, produced in the joint fluid, that form around the affected joint. It is most frequent in men over the age of 35, and its more common names are gout, pseudogout, or gouty arthritis. It is extremely painful and is usually located at the base of the big toe, the instep, the ankle, the knee, and sometimes at the shoulder, wrist, or elbow. People with a strong tendency to develop gout experience as many as five or six attacks a year. Because hyperuricemia (raised uric acid level which causes the formation of the crystals) is partly genetic, the potential for the disease is always present and can never be totally controlled. Drugs such as colchicine, allopurinol, and probenacid are very effective, though. Gout attacks return when the measures to control the patient's uric-acid levels are stopped.

Joint Infection   Infection of a joint occurs when bacteria—generally staphylococcus or gonococcus—find their way into the joint fluid. This can happen to either sex at any age and usually affects the knees, hips, and shoulders. Occasionally, tuberculosis bacteria are the cause, and emergency treatment is required. Bacteria may also lodge in the affected joint from an infection elsewhere in the body, an injection previously given, or by direct injury. Arthritis patients with lowered resistance resulting from a serious illness are often victims of joint infection, which must be treated before it spreads to other parts of the body.

Muscle Inflammation   Inflamed muscle tissues are another form of arthritis affecting either sex at any age. The condition, usually treated with Prednisone (a cortisone derivative), is closely associated with polymyalgia rheumatica and polymyosoitis. When the muscle tissue near a joint becomes inflamed, the inflammatory cells injure the muscle fibers. The resulting painful condition is a newly recognized form of arthritis and occurs mostly in people over 50. Its basic cause is unknown, although scientists believe it is related to arterial inflammation. When artery inflammation is found, this disease is potentially severe and is called giant cell arteritis. Extensive muscle weakness accompanies most forms of arteritis.

Cartilage Destruction   Breakdown of the cartilage—the spongy shock absorber for each of the body's joints—often occurs with the wear and tear of aging, sometimes leaving two surfaces of bone in painful contact with each other. There is little or no inflammation, however, and this type of arthritis is called degenerative joint disease, osteoarthritis, or osteoarthrosis. Almost everyone suffers from this to some degree in their later years. A more benign condition than inflammatory arthritis, osteoarthritis occurs mostly in the finger joints, hips, knees, neck, and the lower back. Usually only one part of the body is affected, and there is no morning stiffness or fever involved as is the case in rheumatoid cases.

Local Conditions   Local conditions have names of their own such as bursitis (inflammation of the shoulder or other joint bursae), tennis elbow, back strain, lumbar disc problem, Achilles tendonitis (heel), heel-spur syndrome, sprained ankle, cervical neck strain, frozen shoulder, and carpal tunnel syndrome (affecting the part of the wrist through which the arm- and hand-controlling radial nerve passes). Most of these conditions can be successfully treated when the doctor's orders are followed and the right home therapy is applied.

General Conditions   Some patients arrive in rheumatologist's offices with what they describe as an "aching-all-over" symptom. This condition can happen to people at any age, although it is more common in the 30-to-50 age group. Called fibrositis, this disease is marked by abnormal sleep patterns, morning stiffness, fatigue, and some locally tender spots in addition to the vague body aches. It is, in fact, closely related to improperly relaxed muscles during sleep and to tension headache. Excessive tension of the neck muscles affects many other parts of the body, including the head. The most effective treatment is *exercise*. The basic purpose of such physical therapy is to strengthen the muscles that activate the joints so that the crippling process can be halted. Unused muscles tend to shrink and cause weakness. Any underlying tension problems must be solved as soon as possible, of course, and then a daily exercise schedule can be mapped out, increasing the amount of exercise slowly toward full cardiovascular conditioning. Warm baths help and, for some, a glass of wine at bedtime.

ARTHRITIS TREATMENT CENTERS

The connective tissue diseases (such as rheumatoid arthritis, lupus erythematosis, polymyositis, scleroderma, and polyarteritis) are sometimes called autoimmune or collagen-vascular diseases. They affect many other organs of the body in addition to the musculoskeletal system. Lupus, for example, is a disease of autoantibodies, and rheumatoid arthritis is a systemic disease. Scleroderma (literally meaning "hard skin") is generally treated as a form of arthritis, although it is not truly arthritis but more a matter of circulatory problems in the small blood vessels.

In all of these painful, inhibiting conditions, you can easily understand that it is best to see a specializing rheumatologist when the aches and pains begin to appear. There are new developments occurring frequently in this field and the person most familiar with them is your qualified rheumatologist. With the proper supervision and treatment by a qualified doctor, you will not fall into the hands of unqualified medical con artists; there are (unfortunately) many in the field of arthritis who are ready to exchange your dollars for often dangerous or useless remedies. Do not trust yourself, either, to a general practitioner or internist with a drawer full of pill samples and too little time to devote to arthritis as a sideline. You may not have arthritis at all or you may have a readily treatable form of it, and the rheumatologist is the person who knows exactly what you should be doing about this basically complex condition.

The outstanding hospitals and centers in the United States on the following list are noted for treatment of arthritis.

Alabama   University of Alabama Medical Center
                   619 South 19th Street/University Station
                   Birmingham, AL 35294
                   (205) 934-5306
                   Program Director: Dr. Gene Ball

California   Stanford University Medical Center
                   300 Pasteur Drive
                   Stanford, CA 94305
                   (415) 723-4000
                   Program Director: Dr. James Fries

Connecticut   University of Connecticut Health Center
                   263 Farmington Avenue
                   Farmington, CT 06032
                   (203) 674-2000
                   Program Director: Dr. Naomi Fox Rothfield
                   (Special interest: treatment of lupus)

Florida   Jackson Memorial Hospital
                   1611 N. W. 12th Avenue
                   Miami, FL 33136
                   (305) 325-7429
                   Program Director: Dr. Norman Gottlieb

Illinois   Northwestern University Medical Center
                   250 East Superior Street
                   Chicago, IL 60611
                   (312) 908-8197
                   Program Director: Dr. Frank Schmid

Maryland	Johns Hopkins Hospital 600 North Wolfe Street Baltimore, MD 21205 (301) 955-5000 Program Director: Dr. Douglas Fearon (Special interest: clinical immunology)
Massachusetts	Boston University Arthritis Center University Hospital 88 East Concord Street Boston, MA 02118 (617) 638-8000 Program Director: Dr. Alan Cohen (Special interest: treatment of amyloidosis)
Minnesota	Mayo Clinic 200 S. W. First Street Rochester, MN 55905 (507) 284-2511 Program Director: Dr. Grene C. Hunder
	University of Minnesota Hospitals Harvard Street at East River Road Minneapolis, MN 55455 (612) 626-3000 Program Director: Dr. Ronald Messner
New York	Hospital for Special Surgery 535 East 70th Street New York, NY 10021 (212) 606-1000 Program Director: Dr. Philip Wilson, Jr. (Designated a multipurpose arthritis center by the National Institutes of Health.)
	St. Luke's Hospital Arthritis Clinic Amsterdam Avenue at 114th Street New York, NY 10025 (212) 870-6000 Program Director: Dr. Stanley Cortell
North Carolina	Duke University Medical Center Box 3005 Durham, NC 27710 (919) 684-5587 Program Director: Dr. Barton F. Haynes

Pennsylvania	Temple University Hospital 3401 North Broad Street Philadelphia, PA 19140 (215) 221-2000 Program Director: Dr. Charles Tourtelotte
	University Health Center of Pittsburgh 121 Meyran Avenue Pittsburgh, PA 15260 (412) 647-2345 Program Director: Dr. Thomas A. Medsger (Special interests: treatment of scleroderma, rheuma- toid arthritis)
South Carolina	Medical University Hospital 171 Ashley Avenue Charleston, NC 29425 (803) 792-3131 Program Director: Dr. E. C. LeRoy (Special interests: treatment of scleroderma, pro- gressive systemic sclerosis)
Virginia	University of Virginia Hospital Jefferson Park Avenue Charlottesville, VA 22908 (804) 924-0211 Program Director: Dr. John Staige Davis IV
Washington	University Hospital of Washington Medical Center 1959 N. E. Pacific Street Seattle, WA 98195 (206) 543-3414 Program Director: Dr. Mart Mannik (Special interests: pediatric and juvenile arthritis)

The preceding list in no way detracts from the good work of hundreds of local arthritis clinics and therapy centers in all parts of the country. For information on arthritis specialists and centers in your area, write to:

> National Arthritis Foundation
> 1314 Spring Street, N. W.
> Atlanta, GA 30309
> (404) 872-7011

There are also offices of this organization in every state (sometimes several in one state). They furnish information and news pamphlets and sponsor programs and local events to keep arthritic people apprised of all new developments in the field.

DIABETES

Most of us think of the pancreas—if we think of it at all—as a large organ located somewhere near the liver and the stomach. The pancreas, in fact, is one of the most important parts of the body. It is the gland that produces insulin, which is a crucial hormone needed to regulate the amount of sugar the body uses for energy. When the pancreas fails to furnish enough insulin from its beta cells, diabetes—the disease of pancreatic failure and the resulting inability to regulate blood sugar levels—occurs.

"In most adults the cause of diabetes appears to be related to beta cells (in the pancreas) running out of insulin," reports Dr. James W. Anderson, professor of medicine and clinical nutrition at the University of Kentucky Medical College, in his book, *Diabetes*. "The best way to combat a tendency to develop diabetes is to eat sensibly. Overeating and carrying too much weight wastes the body's insulin, while staying slim and eating the right foods can stave off a gradual slide into a diabetic state."

The tendency to develop diabetes is, in most cases, inherited, although if the pancreas has been injured, diabetes will then result because insulin is not being produced in the bloodstream and sugar level control is not taking place. Other causes of diabetes are excessive alcohol over long periods (which destroys the pancreas) and viral infections—particularly mumps or flu viruses in children. Diabetes occurs most frequently among overweight or obese people and is 50 percent more common among women than men.

If it is recommended by your personal physician, insulin may be self-injected to help regulate your blood-sugar levels. In fact, under the careful guidance of a doctor, diabetics can learn to monitor their own insulin and dietary needs—both major parts of a daily regime. In addition, the diabetic must know how and when to test urine samples for sugar levels as well as how to adjust a personal life-style to accommodate these processes and the prescribed daily diets. Diabetes may lead to kidney failure, blindness, nerve destruction, and other serious effects if the early symptoms of the disease are ignored.

Among the symptoms of diabetes are extreme thirst, fatigue, too-frequent urination (particularly at night), and slow healing of wounds. By checking early with your personal physician, you may save yourself from more complex forms of treatment later. But rest assured: A diabetic person can lead a healthful and productive life by meticulously following the doctor's orders.

New developments in treatment include pancreas transplant operations, but although diabetes can be cured with a successful transplant, very few medical centers are now equipped to do this procedure. (See chapter 5, "Transplants".)

Currently, technologists in several medical centers in the United States are perfecting small insulin-infusion pumps that automatically deliver precise amounts of insulin at the correct times. Certain versions of this device, which can be worn on a belt, are being used in many parts of the world. American researchers are also in the process of building insulin-infusion pumps capable of delivering the insulin directly into the vein because this is far more effective and predictable.

Among other developments in experimental diabetes laboratories is the injection of pancreatic cells into the body so that diabetics may someday live without insulin injections. Also, experiments are being conducted whereby patients are injected with a substance designed to kill disease-producing cells without injuring the body or an antibody compound to prevent the disease from developing in people prone to diabetes. For further information, call your local chapter of the Juvenile Diabetes Foundation, or the executive offices in New York: (212) 889-7575.

The diabetic patient, meanwhile, must rely upon a carefully chosen doctor, the laboratory team involved with individual testing, and the correct diet to maintain his or her health. In a sense, the diabetic becomes a doctor-at-home in monitoring a lifetime disease, and must often be a dietitian and cook to maintain the all-important nutritional balance.

For information on diabetes treatment throughout the United States, write to:

> American Diabetes Association
> 505 8th Avenue
> New York, NY 10018
> (212) 947-9707

In addition, the following medical centers are among those that have received grants for the funding of research and treatment of diabetes.

Florida

Shands Hospital—University of Florida
1600 S. W. Archer Road
Gainesville, FL 32610
(904) 395-0111

Georgia

Emory University Hospital
1364 Clifton Road, N. E.
Atlanta, GA 30322
(404) 727-7021

Massachusetts

Joslin Clinic
One Joslin Place
Boston, MA 02115
(617) 732-2400

North Carolina

Duke University Medical Center
Box 3005
Durham, NC 27710
(919) 684-5587

MIGRAINE HEADACHES

For anyone who has ever had a migraine attack—and they are counted in the millions—there is no mistaking it for a simple headache. Migraines are generally preceded by a peculiar sort of visual "fireworks display" consisting of double vision, partial blindness, flashing-light shapes, and other eyesight changes. A short while later (usually long enough to allow the subject to stop what he or she is doing and perhaps make it home to the bedroom), severe nausea and vomiting take over along with an almost literally blinding headache on the side of the head, on top, in the front, or in the back. The sufferer is unable to endure light, noise, and other disturbances. This whole headache cycle generally lasts, in severe attacks, 24 hours or more.

Although there are no reliable statistics on the proportion of the population with the chronic condition of migraine (formerly referred to as sick headache) the currently accepted estimate is about 20 percent. It is thought, too, that the reason more women have migraines than do men is because females have many more hormonal changes during their lifetimes.

Despite decades of intensive study of migraine and its causes, the biochemical mechanism that results in a typical migraine attack is so complex that conclusions have yet to be drawn. It is generally agreed among expert researchers, however, that the severe pain of migraine is related closely to the dilation and stretching of blood vessels. Through urine analysis of migraine subjects during an attack, it has also been learned that abnormally high amounts of serotonin (an amine manufactured by the body) appear in the body prior to the pain and then drop to a very low level during the attack. This amine is known to cause dilation of blood vessels as well as to influence mood or behavior.

It is interesting to note that the serotonin produced in the body is stored in disk-shaped microscopic structures in the bloodstream called platelets. Their chief function is to clot the blood and control bleeding. Exactly why the blood platelets in migraine sufferers release more serotonin into the blood is not yet known, but it is thought that when serotonin levels drop suddenly during a migraine attack, blood vessels in the scalp rebound from a constricted state, causing the pain that follows.

Chronic migraine is now recognized as an inherited vascular disorder—*not* a neurotic condition. Therefore, it is unlikely that the cure for a migraine headache will be found until the many questions about its chemical background are answered.

Because of the interaction of elements in the bloodstream during a migraine attack, strong painkiller drugs such as codeine have little effect on the migraine, although they do help the sufferer sleep.

Meanwhile—as research continues—here are some helpful tips from *How to Find Relief from Migraine* by Rosemary Dudley, executive vice president and founder of the Migraine Foundation of Toronto, Canada, and journalist Wade Rowland.

1. Try to identify the food items, if any, that trigger your migraine attacks. Among foodstuffs known to bring on attacks in a large percentage of migraine patients are chocolate, aged cheese and dairy products, citrus fruits, nondairy coffee creamers, alcoholic drinks, fatty fried foods, vegetables (especially onions), meat (especially pork), seafood, tea, and coffee.

2. Establish regular sleep and meal patterns. Too much sleep frequently triggers a migraine, and no migraine sufferer should go more than five hours without food intake. Avoid frequent use of sleeping pills except following surgery or emotional shock. Natural sleep is good for migraine victims; drug-induced sleep between attacks can often increase the incidence of migraine attacks.

3. Avoid sunlight and glare by wearing sunglasses. Lightly tinted glasses should be used to cut down the glare from oncoming headlights when driving at night. Contact lenses should be removed if you feel an impending attack, since both eyeballs begin to swell and can cause harmful pressure.

4. To offset the effects of noise, a well-known trigger of migraine attacks, keep a set of earplugs in your pocket. Noisy offices can be made more pleasant for migraine sufferers with the use of newly available plastic shields for office typewriters.

5. Avoid the steam from cooking large family meals, often a migraine trigger for some susceptible individuals. (Tip: cook the turkey a day or two in advance of the holiday or buy one already cooked.)

6. Avoid unusual motion such as on a cruise ship, accompanying a child on a carnival ferris wheel, and so on.

7. For the victims of chronic migraine, plan trips that can be taken in easy stages and will allow you to maintain your sleep and food schedules. Also, ask the pharmacist to label migraine prescriptions "For migraine" and perhaps carry a "To whom it may concern" letter from your physician to present to customs agents or foreign hospitals.

Among the leading centers for the treatment of migraines are:

California

California Medical Clinic for Headache
16542 Ventura Boulevard
Encino, CA 91436
(818) 986-4248
Program Director: Dr. Lee Kudrow

Scripps Clinic Medical Group, Inc.
10666 North Torey Pines Road
La Jolla, CA 92037
(619) 455-9100
Program Director: Dr. Donald Dalessio

Connecticut   New England Center for Headache
                       40 East Putnam Avenue
                       Cos Cob, CT 06807
                       (203) 968-1799
                       Program Directors: Dr. Alan Rapoport
                                          Dr. Fred Sheftell

Michigan   Michigan Headache and Neurological Center
                       3120 Professional Drive
                       Ann Arbor, MI 48109
                       (313) 973-1155
                       Program Director: Dr. Joel Saper

In addition, the following organization furnishes medical information on migraine:

                       National Headache Foundation
                       5252 North Western Avenue
                       Chicago, IL 60625
                       (312) 878-7715
                       Program Director: Suzanne Simons

PARKINSON'S DISEASE

Named after Dr. James Parkinson, an English physician of the early nineteenth century, Parkinson's disease (sometimes called Parkinson's syndrome) was once known as paralysis agitans or shaking palsy. An estimated 2.5 million Americans have this degenerative, debilitating, and progressive disease of the central nervous system, which originates in the brain's thalamus. It is characterized by a slowly spreading tremor, muscular weakness, rigidity (when affecting the face it's called Parkinson's mask), and a peculiar, shuffling gait. The onset can be abrupt, then gradually affect other parts of the body. There is little chance of complete recovery.

A number of medicines exist that combat the tremors, the rigidity, and the lethargy of this disease, and there is a special therapy that can halt tremors for a time through the application of extreme cold to a small part of the thalamus. Also, there is the drug, L-dopa, which has helped alleviate symptoms for many.

If you or someone close to you is showing early symptoms of Parkinson's (such as a shaking hand or foot) seek the best neurologist for a diagnosis. Remember: Parkinson's medications are intended only to affect symptoms; if the medications are not accomplishing their purpose in an individual case, a change in the amount of medication prescribed or a new diagnosis may be needed.

The National Parkinson Foundation, under the clinical direction of Dr. William J. Weiner, is affiliated with the department of neurology of the University of Miami School of Medicine. As such, it provides patients coming to the foundation the opportunity of diagnostic evaluation by neurologists who are experts in the treatment of Parkinson's disease as well as other neurological disorders. As a one-of-a-kind institution, the foundation is also in the forefront of clinical research programs evaluating recent drugs such as pergolide (direct-acting dopamine receptor), amantadine, and cogentine for patients in the early stages of the disease.

National Parkinson Foundation, Inc.
1501 N. W. Ninth Avenue
Miami, FL 33136
(305) 547-6666
Program Director: Dr. William Weiner

· 9 ·
PEDIATRICS: CARING FOR THE YOUNGEST PATIENTS

Pediatrics is the total care of young humanity—from birth (or even earlier) until about the age of 18. From a specialty that 50 years ago was concerned mainly with the treatment of childhood infections, and from much uncertainty about the nutritional requirements of the growing child, pediatrics has blossomed into a multidisciplinary array of specialties. (A number of pediatric medical centers on our selected list have 25 to 30 subdivisions concerned with the medical and surgical care of infants and children, even though we have limited our research to only a few main subdivisions.) Cooperation of one specialty with another, of research scientists with clinicians, and of pediatrics with other branches of medicine, while keeping the needs of the individual patient foremost in mind, is the principal force in saving countless human lives that were formerly lost to unknown causes or "failure to thrive."

Neonatology deals with premature babies who may have a multitude of problems and full-term babies with such problems as pneumonia, congenital defects, and genetic diseases. Prematurity accounts for most of the problems of early life and is, in fact, one of the principal public health problems. The neonatologist is increasingly concerned with what goes on before birth. A sophisticated Preterm Birth Prevention Program, which closely monitors mothers at risk of premature labor, was designed by Dr. Robert K. Creasy, chief of obstetrics and gynecology at the University of Texas Medical School in Houston. The program recognizes 95 percent of high-risk patients and 75 percent of low-risk patients in time for them to be treated successfully. Constant communication between patient and doctor in the critical period, education of the mother in what to look for, and use of the labor-stopping drug ritodrine are the basis of successful prevention of prematurity. Clinics having this program are

University of California, San Francisco, where Dr. Creasy developed the program; University of California, San Diego; Vanderbilt University in Nashville, Tennessee; Northwestern University in Evanston, Illinois; the University of Alabama in Birmingham; Ohio State University in Columbus; and University of Texas-Southwestern in Dallas.

There has been a tremendous application of new technology in the area of intensive care for newborns. This is happily illustrated by the fact that of babies with birth weights of 1.6 to 2.2 pounds treated in Stanford University Medical Center's intensive-care nursery, 75 percent survive. "And," says the associate director of the unit, Dr. David Stevenson, "information gathered over the last 20 years—even before we had the kind of survival rate achieved over the past three years—leads us to believe that most of the babies in this very low birth-weight group go on to be normal." It is now possible to custom-tailor the nutritional requirements of premature babies and of older infants requiring intensive-care treatment to reduce the risk of infection and help overcome respiratory problems.

The dietary and nutritional requirements of both sick and healthy infants— once the subject of endless controversy—seems to have been settled. The right amounts of vitamins required under various conditions are now well known.

The weight of opinion in another controversial question, cow's milk versus mother's milk, is currently in favor of the latter, especially for preterm infants. Breast-feeding, however, is recognized as having limitations for some employed mothers and for others who cannot always accommodate it to their life-styles. Physical inability to breast-feed accounts for very few failures. Most important in this case is the support provided for the mother by physicians and family members.

Accumulation of bile pigment (bilirubin), toxic to brain nerve cells, is another problem of some premature infants, babies of diabetic mothers, and those with certain anemias. Some must have blood transfusions, but most are simply placed under white lights, with black patches protecting their eyes. This light is most effective in breaking down bilirubin.

Pediatric cardiology was pioneered in the United States by the late Drs. Helen B. Taussig and Alfred Blalock of Johns Hopkins Hospital, who worked out a classification of congenital and other heart diseases of children. Ten years before open-heart surgery was possible, they also devised an operation to help "blue babies." This problem was caused by the failure of a duct (normally open in fetal life to shunt blood away from the lungs) to close in early life and allow blood to be oxygenated in the lungs; this duct, outside the heart, was tied off, and the blue babies became pink.

Another heart problem some newborns must contend with is the failure of the heart to develop properly. Nature provides a hole between the right and left sides of the heart (another bypass of the lungs, which are underdeveloped and nonfunctioning in fetal life) which gradually closes shortly after birth and is almost, if not quite entirely, sealed by the age of one year. When this hole fails to close, abnormal mixtures of oxygenated and venous blood results. In premature babies the circulatory problems are naturally more severe, sometimes leading to congestive failure as the lungs become flooded with too much blood. When drugs are unable to close the hole, the child may require heart surgery.

Added to these defects are numerous combinations of one or more imperfections involving heart valves, the position or attachment of major blood vessels to the heart, enlargement of the heart muscle, and the size of its chambers and communicating vessels. Many problems, formerly life-threatening, are being successfully treated by open-heart surgery in one or more stages. In all cases, accurate diagnosis of the type and extent of the defect(s) is a must; this is being facilitated by refinements in magnetic resonance imaging (MRI) and other technology. A small number of children, sometimes quite young, are afflicted with heart diseases (such as coronary artery disease) that are much more common in the older population. Rheumatic heart disease, formerly the most common heart ailment in children, is still seen, although less frequently because the causal Group-A streptococcal infections are now promptly treated with appropriate antibiotics.

Another area of specialty is pediatric endocrinology. Most bodily functions are regulated by hormones manufactured by the endocrine glands. Over- or underproduction of these hormones gives rise to numerous diseases of varying degrees of disability. The pituitary gland, in addition to certain functions of its own, is the master gland that regulates some functions of the other endocrine glands. Clearly, normal growth and development of children depends upon the recognition and treatment of any endocrine abnormality. Two of the many areas of importance in this regard are physical stature and diabetes. The introduction of pituitary growth hormone, for example, can spur human growth where its lack is the cause of the disorder. The National Pituitary Agency, a division of the National Institutes of Health, distributes the limited supply of this hormone to physicians specializing in basic and clinical research in this field. One program, at the University of Florida in Gainesville under the direction of Dr. Arland Rosenbloom, is achieving growth rates of three inches per year in selected patients.

Comparatively few centers on our list have departments in the subspecialty of pediatric nephrology. Research that formerly focused on how the whole kidney works has undergone a transition, with much more emphasis now on how the individual parts of the kidney work at the cellular and molecular level. Although most kidney disorders that affect adults may be seen in children, certain childhood kidney diseases (either having their origin in the kidneys or in diseases of other bodily parts that prominently affect the kidney) require the expertise of pediatric nephrologists. These disorders involve congenital abnormalities of structure and function, abnormal variations in blood supply to the kidney, benign and malignant tumors, the effects of certain toxic substances, and kidney reactions to the stress of surgical operations or burns, to mention but a few of the main conditions encountered.

Both children and their parents must be helped to adjust to the varying degrees of psychological stress that accompany most severe illnesses, especially those that require long convalescence resulting from a series of operations or medical treatments. Many of the programs in the neurobiological sciences are aimed at the discovery of physical and biological causes of genetic diseases, hormonal and metabolic disorders, and abnormal circulatory patterns, with their possible effects upon the brain. Sophisticated programs for the understanding and treatment of autistic children have been developed as well as other programs for those with learning disabilities. Emphasis is upon prevention, where possible, of disabling psychiatric conditions. Programs for the treatment of children increasingly include family treatment.

Although we recognize that excellent work is done in some centers without formal programs in pediatric surgery but with surgeons who have pediatric surgical training performing in the surgical subspecialties, there is a distinct advantage in having children undergo surgery of any type in those centers that have departments of pediatric surgery.

California

Children's Hospital of Los Angeles
4650 Sunset Boulevard
Los Angeles, CA 90027
(213) 660-2450
Program Director (pediatric medicine): Dr. Eliot W. Nelson
Program Director (pediatric surgery): Dr. Morton W. Woolley

University of California Los Angeles Medical Center
10833 Le Conte Avenue
Los Angeles, CA 90024
(213) 825-9111
Program Director: Dr. Arthur Moss

Children's Hospital at Stanford
520 Willow Road
Palo Alto, CA 94304
(415) 327-4800
Program Director: Dr. Irving Schulman

Colorado

Children's Hospital
1056 East 19th Avenue
Denver, CO 80218
(303) 329-3066
Program Drector: Dr. Frederick Battaglia

Connecticut

Yale–New Haven Hospital
333 Cedar Street
New Haven, CT 06510
(203) 785-4242
Program Director: Dr. Norman Siegel

District of *Columbia*	Children's Hospital National Medical Center 111 Michigan Avenue, N. W. Washington, DC 20010 (202) 745-5000 Program Director (pediatric medicine): Dr. Arnold 　Einhorn Program Director (pediatric surgery): Dr. Judson 　Randolph
Florida	Shands Hospital—University of Florida 1600 S. W. Archer Road Gainesville, FL 32610 (904) 395-0111 Program Director: Dr. Robert Parkhurst Nemours Children's Hospital 5720 Atlantic Boulevard Jacksonville, FL 32207 (904) 390-3600 Program Director (pediatric medicine): Dr. Prentiss E. 　Findlay Program Director (pediatric surgery): Dr. H. Warner 　Webb
Illinois	Children's Memorial Hospital 2300 Children's Plaza Chicago, IL 60614 (312) 880-4549 Program Director (pediatric medicine): Dr. James 　Stockman III Program Director (pediatric surgery): Dr. John 　Raffensperger
Indiana	Indiana University Medical Center 926 West Michigan Street Indianapolis, IN 46223 (317) 635-8431 Program Director: Dr. Morris Green
Iowa	University of Iowa Hospitals and Clinics 650 Newton Road Iowa City, IA 52242 (319) 356-0469 Program Director: Dr. Frank Morriss

Maryland

Johns Hopkins Hospital
600 North Wolfe Street
Baltimore, MD 21205
(301) 955-5000
Program Director (pediatric medicine): Dr. Catherine
De Angelis
Program Director (pediatric surgery): Dr. J.
Alexander Haller, Jr.

Massachusetts

Children's Hospital
300 Longwood Avenue
Boston, MA 02115
(617) 735-6000
Program Director (pediatric medicine): Dr. David
Nathan
Program Director (pediatric surgery): Dr. Raphael
Levey

Michigan

C. S. Mott Children's Hospital
1505 Simpson Road East
Ann Arbor, MI 48109
(313) 764-1573
Program Director: Dr. Arnold G. Coran

Minnesota

University of Minnesota Hospitals
Harvard Street at East River Road
Minneapolis, MN 55455
(612) 624-4477
Program Director: Dr. Alfred F. Michael

Mayo Clinic
200 S. W. First Street
Rochester, MN 55905
(507) 284-2511
Program Director: Dr. Gerald S. Gilchrist

Missouri

St. Louis Children's Hospital
400 South Kingshighway Boulevard
St. Louis, MO 63178
(314) 454-6000
Program Director: Dr. James Keating

New York   Children's Hospital of Buffalo
                      219 Bryant Street
                      Buffalo, NY 14222
                      (716) 878-7000
                      Program Director (pediatric medicine): Dr. Robert E.
                        Cooke
                      Program Director (pediatric surgery): Dr. Donald
                        Cooney

                      Columbia-Presbyterian Medical Center
                      622 West 168th Street
                      New York, NY 10032
                      (212) 305-2500
                      Program Director (pediatric medicine): Dr. Michael
                        Katz
                      Program Director (pediatric surgery): Dr. R. Peter
                        Altman

                      State University Hospital–Downstate Medical Center
                      445 Lenox Road
                      New York, NY 11203
                      (718) 270-2401
                      Program Director (pediatric medicine): Dr. Laurence
                        Fineberg
                      Program Director (pediatric surgery): Dr. Peter
                        Kottmeier

                      New York Hospital–Cornell Medical Center
                      525 East 68th Street
                      New York, NY 10021
                      (212) 472-5454
                      Program Directors: Dr. John Ferry
                                         Dr. Lewis Reisman

                      Strong Memorial Hospital
                      601 Elmwood Avenue
                      Rochester, NY 14642
                      (716) 275-2951
                      Program Director: Dr. Robert Hoekelman

North Carolina   Duke University Medical Center
                      Box 3005
                      Durham, NC 27710
                      (919) 684-5587
                      Program Director: Dr. Laura Gutman

North Carolina Memorial Hospital
Manning Drive
Chapel Hill, NC 27514
(919) 966-4131
Program Director: Dr. Thomas Boat

Ohio

Children's Hospital Medical Center
Elland and Bethesda Avenues
Cincinnati, OH 45229
(513) 559-4200
Program Director (pediatric medicine): Dr. William
    Schubert
Program Director (pediatric surgery): Dr. Lester
    Martin

University Hospitals of Cleveland
2074 Abington Road
Cleveland, OH 44106
(216) 444-1000
Program Director: Dr. William Speck

Children's Hospital
700 Children's Drive
Columbus, OH 43205
(614) 461-2000
Program Director (pediatric medicine): Dr. Delphis
    Richardson
Program Director (pediatric surgery): Dr. Thomas
    Boles, Jr.

Oregon

Oregon Health Science University Hospital
3181 West Sam Jackson Park Road
Portland, OR 97201
(503) 225-8311
Program Director: Dr. Stephen Lafranchi

Pennsylvania

Children's Hospital of Philadelphia
34th Street at Civic Center Boulevard
Philadelphia, PA 19104
(215) 596-9100
Program Director (pediatric medicine): Dr. Richard B
    Johnston
Program Director (pediatric surgery): Dr. James
    O'Neill, Jr.

St. Christopher's Hospital for Children
Fifth Street and Lehigh Avenue
Philadelphia, PA 19133
(215) 427-5000
Program Director (pediatric medicine): Dr. Iain F.
  Bleck
Program Director (pediatric surgery): Dr. William
  Weintraub

Children's Hospital of Pittsburgh
125 De Sota Street
Pittsburgh, PA 15213
(412) 692-5700
Program Director (pediatric medicine): Dr. J. Carlton
  Gartner
Program Director (pediatric surgery): Dr. Marc Rowe

Tennessee   LeBonheur Children's Medical Center
848 Adams Avenue
Memphis, TN 38103
(901) 522-3000
Program Director: Dr. Henry G. Herrod

Vanderbilt University Hospital
1211 22nd Avenue, South
Nashville, TN 37232
(615) 322-7311
Program Director: Dr. David Karzon

Texas   Texas Children's Hospital
6621 Fannin Street
Houston, TX 77030
(713) 798-1000
Program Director: Dr. Jan Van Eys

Virginia   University of Virginia Hospital
Jefferson Park Avenue
Charlottesville, VA 22908
(804) 924-0211
Program Director: Dr. Richard Kesler

Washington   Children's Hospital and Medical Center
4800 Sand Point Way, N. E.
Seattle, WA 98105
(206) 526-2000
Program Director (pediatric medicine): Dr. Thomas
  W. Pendergrass
Program Director (pediatric surgery): Dr. David
  Trapper

· 10 ·
GERIATRICS: FACING
THE PROBLEMS OF
OLD AGE

"There is no shortcut to longevity. To win it is the work of a lifetime . . ." said the late Sir James Crichton Brown. So agreed a group of international medical scholars who constituted the editorial board of *Executive Health,* a health-oriented newsletter for top executives. After careful studies of case histories of extraordinarily long-lived individuals, the scholars and research scientists involved concluded (1) the so-called diseases of old age essentially affect the "dangerous years"—50 to 70—and (2) in all the case histories, seven constants emerged from each life pattern of those individuals studied. These seven constants are cheerfulness, good heredity, physical activity, good health, self-imposed discipline, hard work at projects they enjoy, and emotional stability. Luck, of course, plays a role in determining longevity, but the years after 50 are a time to begin changing unhealthy life-styles.

In 1974 the Congress of the United States mandated the establishment of the National Institute on Aging (NIA), a division of the National Institutes of Health. Shortly thereafter, the first professorship in geriatric medicine was established at Cornell University Medical Center in Manhattan. Now gerontology is part of the curriculum at many medical colleges, and a great deal is being done about the universally recognized American fear of growing old.

Although at present there is little that we can do about what gerontologists call "primary" or chronological aging, there is a great deal that can be done to slow the process of "secondary" aging (resulting from the sum of all the stresses to which a person is subject). Our best weapons in this fight are certain changes we can make in our daily lives.

Nutrition alone, according to researchers at the NIA, accounts in large part for the longevity of the centenarians discovered in remote corners of the world. The two things these scattered people have in common are a frugal diet and hard physical work.

Although proper nutrition is important to the process of maintaining a healthy body, few Americans adhere to the protective "eat less" dietary rules. As a nation, we still have far more than our share of obese people. But here is an experiment we should all remember when we are tempted to overeat. Dr. Clive McCay, a Cornell University gerontologist in the 1920s, fed one group of rats a balanced diet and another group one-third the same amount. The second group of rats came close, according to the report, to doubling the life span of the first group that was fed larger portions.

Exercise, which helps the brain and body resist disease-triggering aging by aiding the body's immune system, also keeps the whole bodily system in prime condition. Most of us, unfortunately, tend to forget not only that exercise helps resist primary aging but also that the unexercised body deteriorates rapidly. NASA studies show, for example, that for every three days of immobility, a person loses one-fifth of total body strength. Regular, structured exercise (within individual limits) will do more to preserve the quality of your life than any other change you can make in your life-style.

There are some antiaging drugs and treatments available today, and many more are due in the not-too-distant future. Oxygen therapy, for example, shows some promise in recharging the memories of older persons, and a chemical has been found by Dr. Robert Kohn of Case–Western Reserve University that inhibits the cross-linkage of collagen in the skin—long suspected as the cause of skin wrinkling.

Meanwhile, middle-aged men and women in droves are taking advantage—when they can afford it—of plastic surgery to remove the facial lines, sags, and wrinkles of aging. In a youth-worshipping world, in fact, the process may be thought necessary to hold a job or to get a new one.

For women especially, "middle age"—roughly between the 40s and early 50s—also brings menopause, when the ovaries cease producing the important female hormones estrogen and progesterone. Although lifetime estrogen replacement therapy, introduced by many noted gynecologists (especially the late Dr. Robert E. Wilson, of King's County Hospital in New York City) in the early 1960s, was hailed as a panacea, it stirred up a great deal of controversy. Quite simply, this is a prescribed regimen of hormone pills (preferably nonsynthetic) taken on a monthly schedule to prolong love life, work life, and whatever kind of life the patient wants to lead. It is now, however, considered a necessity by many gynecologists for pre- and post-menopause protection of women against osteoporosis (brittle bones) and a number of other factors in feminine vitality loss.

In addition to the estrogen replacement school of medical thought, the American Society for Bone and Mineral Research has drafted the following guidelines for everyone (especially women) to prevent or slow down osteoporosis:

• Participate in daily exercise, especially running or walking; bones, like muscles, wither with disuse.

- Maintain a calcium-rich diet (800 to 1,000 milligrams of calcium a day) and two full glasses of milk.
- Avoid excessive doses of vitamins A and D.
- Don't smoke! Studies show that smoking clogs blood vessels that nourish the bony skeleton.

Although the majority of women undergoing normal menopause may welcome the postmenopausal period of their lives as a time of freedom from the fears of pregnancy and the periodic discomforts they have endured during their adult lives, most of these women are also likely to forget about the continuing need to see their gynecologists—at least an annual physical checkup. As a protection against cancer of the cervix, the Pap smear is crucial, and the correct regimen of estrogen therapy will give women added protection against the danger of brittle bones, "dowager's hump," and crippled spines.

Middle-aged men, too, have their own problems at this stage of life, although for the most part they are mainly psychological. Sometimes called mid-life crisis or male menopause, the tendency to embark on totally different careers and break up formerly stable marriages can and does happen to many men in their late 40s and early 50s. As one man puts it, "The urge to prove you are still a young man and a Beau Brummel is sometimes uncontrollable."

But also important at this period is the beginning of the enlargement of the prostate gland located near the rectum. If not attended to by a skilled urologist (see chapter 4, "Surgery," for the listing of urology centers of note), the enlarged prostate creates obstructions, can become cancerous, and usually must be removed or treated. Such a procedure, it should be emphasized, requires great surgical skill owing to the prostate's sensitive location near important nerves. Do not hesitate to choose the best, most experienced urological care available to you—even if it means traveling to obtain it. The quality of the life remaining may depend completely on a wise choice of the most experienced urological surgeon you can find.

"Old age" is an outmoded category of the dim past, in which few American "oldsters" put themselves today. Instead they have become "senior citizens," living in "retirement communities" and—thanks to modern medicine or heredity or both—leading active lives. Frequently they are managing their own homes at an advanced age, and the list of 100-year-old men and women grows a little longer every year. When senior parents or close relatives become seriously ill and in need of nursing care, however, they are usually placed in nursing homes. The quality of care available is wide-ranging, and most families today—no matter how caring—are not equipped to care for the special needs of the very ill old person who must at long last arrive at the hospitalization stage.

With few exceptions, the day of the elderly rich with the wherewithal to pay for private 24-hour nursing care is past. Even when possible, the strain of adapting family living to a round-the-clock nursing routine is difficult, if not insurmountable. Then the nursing home becomes the only viable alternative.

Therefore, if you—like most people—have an older family member who may be needing institutional care sometime soon, you should take the time to investigate the nursing homes in areas within easy visiting range. The quality of care, the cost, nutrition, and attractiveness should all be subjected to on-site inspection. Do not take the word of a brochure or even of a well-meaning friend. Nursing homes can run the gamut from the downright disgraceful to the high-priced "convalescent centers." In general, religious organizations can furnish lists of surrounding area nursing homes they sponsor, and name others which are religiously affiliated. But do not wait until an emergency situation forces you to make a hasty, ill-considered choice. Nursing homes can be cheerful and some are arranged so that patients can be placed in accommodations according to their degree of illness.

If you know in advance what to expect and where to find it, the transition from home to nursing home or from hospital to convalescent-care center can be smoother for both you and the patient. By setting up in advance a savings fund for what can be a realistic and costly matter, you may save yourself and your family great financial uncertainty.

In the meantime, there are many organizations in almost every community dedicated to the welfare and happiness of the elderly person, who should be encouraged to seek the much-needed companionship of contemporaries. For example, the Heritage Home Health agency in Bristol, New Hampshire, videotapes clients for a home-sharing plan called "People Match." In this plan, a client lacking physical health but having ample means often teams up with another person with no money but who is able to do light housework.

For other ideas and answers to many of the problems of the elderly, write to:

National Institute on Aging
Bldg. 31, Room 5 C-36
Bethesda, MD 20205

Request reprints of the "Age Page" bulletin they put out for this purpose. Be sure to specify the subject in which you are interested.

As a final suggestion to interested families of difficult-to-treat elderly persons, there are approximately 400 psychiatrists throughout the country whose specialty is treatment of elderly patients. Your county medical society or branch of the American Medical Association can furnish the names and addresses of these doctors.

· 11 ·
SOCIAL DISEASES OF
NEW IMPORTANCE

THE CLASSIC VENEREAL DISEASES

Syphilis and gonorrhea—probably as old as mankind—are the two classic venereal diseases. The early stages of these two diseases can usually be cured by antimicrobial drugs, thus preventing their destructive consequences. They are, however, sometimes difficult to diagnose, particularly in the female, and may go undetected until the effects are all too apparent. At times, resistance of the causative microorganisms to the usually effective antibiotics complicates the treatment and allows the disease to advance. They are, therefore, contagious and epidemic. Persons who suspect they have acquired such diseases are urged to seek immediate medical attention for their own and their partners' protection. Public health departments are well equipped to manage medical treatment of these diseases and also to encourage the examination and treatment of contacts.

HERPES

Herpes of the genitals is caused by a variant of the virus herpes simplex which, on the lips or surrounding skin, produces the familiar fever blister or cold sore that nearly everyone experiences at some time or other. The virus, present in the tissues of the body, is normally controlled by the immune system and becomes symptomatic only when these protective forces become depleted—often by other diseases or by medicines employed for their control.

Genital herpes is spread by persons harboring the virus to those whose immunity is low. It does not follow that a person will develop herpes *because* of contact with one who harbors the virus. Diagnosis in the male is usually obvious from the characteristic red, painful, hivelike sore on the penis. The active lesion in the female may go undetected if it is hidden from view. In either case, the sore, similar to a fever blister, lasts a week or more and then disappears. If immunity remains low, there is a tendency to recurrence. More often than not, individuals go through stages when the virus flares up followed by months or perhaps several years without any evidence of its activity. Improvement of general health should favorably affect the immune system.

The effect of an antiviral drug, acyclovir, applied as an ointment to the active lesions of herpes, does soothe and greatly shorten the course of the acute herpetic sore, but it does nothing to prevent recurrence and apparently has no general effect upon the immune system.

Aside from the discomfort of the sores, sometimes severe and long-lasting, there are usually no ill effects of genital herpes upon persons harboring the virus. Serious difficulties may occur, however, when a pregnant woman has active herpes lesions at the time of delivery of her baby. If the herpes virus is being shed into the birth canal, there is the distinct possibility that the bodily tissues (including the brain) of the baby may be infected. In women with a history of herpes, frequent examinations can allow an estimate of the risk. If the pregnancy is not at term, acyclovir applications may rapidly clear any lesions. If at term, then cesarean-section delivery is necessary.

AIDS

Tragic as it is to contemplate, the latter part of this century may well go down in medical history as the beginning of the world's most devastating epidemic of sexually transmitted disease: AIDS (Acquired Immune Deficiency Syndrome).

The causative agent of AIDS is a virus called Human T-lymphocyte Virus-3 (HTLV-3). Based on variations in the outer core of the virus, 19 separate species of the virus have been identified. AIDS is transmitted directly through sexual contact, by sharing a hypodermic needle with an infected person, by contaminated blood given in transfusions, or through birth. There is no evidence that AIDS is spread through casual social contact; AIDS is acquired only through direct contact with the virus.

The AIDS incubation period (between infection and symptom) can range from a few months to five or more years with no telltale symptoms—among which are night sweats; rapid weight loss; swollen lymph glands in the neck, underarm, or groin areas; and white spots or unsual blemishes in the mouth. AIDS is characterized by a severe general breakdown of the body's immune system, affording little protection against normally mild or rare diseases, which become potentially fatal. The two most common effects are Kaposi's sarcoma, a form of cancer causing brown or purplish skin blotches, and a form of pneumonia caused by the bacterium pneumocystis carinii. New evidence shows that HTLV-3 may also attack the nervous system causing damage to the brain and spinal cord and resulting in memory loss, inability to make decisions, and loss of coordination.

Kaposi's sarcoma is the first human tumor proven to be caused by a virus— probably a genetic variant of the HTLV-3 that causes AIDS, because there appears to be a close relationship between the biological mechanisms involved in the development of AIDS and those responsible for the growth of this tumor. Scientists, including Dr. William A. Haseltine of Harvard Medical School, are investigating viral proteins produced by several types of similar HTLV viruses. Some of these proteins apparently control genes that promote or stop tumor growth. One bright aspect of the gloomy picture of AIDS is that its research may well produce some answers to the cancer problem.

Dr. Jay A. Levy and his coworkers at the University of California, San Francisco, in cooperation with scientists at the Chiron Corporation (a biotechnological company) have succeeded in cloning genetic material from the HTLV-3 virus, work which is essential for the production of a vaccine. But before a workable vaccine can be discovered, more must be known about the genetic codes responsible for the 19 different species of the virus and whether there is a cross-relativity among them. Medical centers at the University of California in both Los Angeles and San Francisco, at Harvard, and at Mt. Sinai Medical Center all have ongoing research programs. One hopeful sign: isoprinosine, a biological modifier that in tests has improved resistance to the HTLV-3 virus (and probably to herpes simplex), has been approved by the Food and Drug Administration for investigational use. Some other treatments are available: The drug interferon has been helpful in treating Kaposi's sarcoma; interleukin 2, a disease-fighting chemical occuring naturally in the body, shows promise in laboratory tests; surgery and radiation have helped in overcoming some AIDS-related symptoms; and the drugs AZT and pentamidine can delay the onset of AIDS symptoms, thereby extending the life of AIDS sufferers.

Because the AIDS situation is so rapidly changing, we have not listed many hospitals here. By now inner-city hospitals are almost all quite experienced in treating AIDS patients. The following can provide valuable information about the disease:

> People with AIDS (PWA) Newsline
> PWA Coalition Inc.
> 31 West 26th Street, 5th floor
> New York, NY 10010
> (212) 532-0290
> Hot line (treatment information and resource referral):
> (212) 532-0568
>
> Gay Men's Health Crisis (GMHC)
> (212) 807-6664
> Hot line: (212) 807-6655

For the latest, most authoritative information on AIDS—its diagnosis, treatment, and current studies in progress—call the National Institutes of Health (NIH) AIDS hot line: (800) 342-AIDS. AIDS patients who want to know what medical studies they can participate in can call Research Clinical Trials: (800) TRIALSA. For the newest publications and literature about AIDS, call the National AIDS Clearing Department of Information : (800) 458-5231.

These medical centers are among the leaders in the search for a cure for AIDS:

California   University of California San Francisco Hospitals and
                      Clinics
                      505 Parnassus Avenue
                      San Francisco, CA 94143
                      (415) 476-1000

                      University of California Los Angeles Medical Center
                      10833 Le Conte Avenue
                      Los Angeles, CA 90024
                      (213) 825-9111

Massachusetts   Massachusetts General Hospital
                      32 Fruit Street
                      Boston, MA 02114
                      (617) 726-2000

New York   Mt. Sinai Hospital
                      One Gustav Levy Place
                      New York, NY 10029
                      (212) 650-6500

· 12 ·
PSYCHIATRY: NEW APPROACHES TO MENTAL ILLNESS

Once thought of as being on the fringes of medicine, psychiatry—the study of the human mind—has earned an important place among the medical specialties.

In addition to a knowledge of general medical care, psychiatrists are now required to have postgraduate training in internal medicine. The old image of "the shrink" and his or her couch is slowly fading from the scene. Today's psychiatrists are more likely to be physicians writing prescriptions to cure or control a patient's biochemical imbalance. Their province, though, is still the extraordinary departures from an individual's routine way of thinking, acting, and feeling.

Temporary departures from a state of emotional equilibrium are common for everyone. For example, exhilaration over some success or triumph, grief over the loss of a loved one, rage over a real or imagined insult, or loss of self-respect and depression when an expected promotion falls through are understandable reactions. When these reactions are prolonged, with adverse effects to the job, family relationships, and to the enjoyment of life, they become serious enough to require the help of a psychiatrist skilled in the diagnosis and treatment of mental disorders.

The great majority of mental illnesses respond to treatment within a comparatively short period of time. As attitudes become more educated, the stigma formerly attached to mental illness shows signs of fading out almost entirely. As more is learned about the chemistry of the nervous system and the brain, it will be only a matter of time before most, if not all, mental illness is explained on the basis of organic causes.

Properly selected and prescribed medicines now form a major part of psychiatric treatment. Although the medicines are not curative in themselves, they often raise the awareness of very sick patients so that they may benefit from other psychotherapeutic modes of treatment. Older ways of treating mental patients, such as electroshock therapy, are still useful in certain cases, but there is now a great deal more emphasis on group therapy, family therapy, intermediate types of residential care (between hospital and home), preventive psychiatry, and the encouragement of reasonable attitudes in the community toward the mentally ill—especially on the part of employers.

"It has been estimated that one out of every five persons over eighteen years of age suffers from a recognizable form of bi-polar (manic-depressive) or uni-polar (manic *or* depressive) illness," says Dr. Moke Wayne Williams, ortho-molecular psychiatrist and medical director of the Coral Ridge Psychiatric Hospital in Fort Lauderdale, Florida. In an Afterword to *The Story of J* (an autobiography by Terry Garrity), Dr. Williams, a leading exponent of the "new psychiatry," further states that "biochemical mood swing is a much more significant disease than is generally known. I don't doubt that on any given day we all do business and 'socialize' with one or more manic-depressives or uni-polar depressives, many of whom don't know that they are and so they don't seek professional help. . . . In the past few years, medical science has vastly improved its ability to correctly diagnose and treat biological mood disturbances."

The book suggests that "three or more of the symptoms in the following list, occuring concurrently and lasting two to three weeks would be indicative of a manic episode":

1. Marked increase in energy and sudden involvement in multiple activities.
2. Decreased need for sleep.
3. Overly talkative, abnormally gregarious.
4. Physically restless.
5. Unable to concentrate, easily distractible.
6. Racing thoughts, flights of ideas.
7. Inflated sense of power, knowledge, or self-importance.
8. Inappropriate laughing.
9. Unwarranted optimism.
10. Reckless driving.
11. Increased sexual activity, perhaps infidelities.
12. Wild spending sprees.
13. Hyperirritability; burst of anger.
14. Indiscriminate giving away of money or possessions.
15. Delusions.
16. Lack of concern for consequences of acts.

Indicating a "depressive episode," four or more of the following symptoms lasting one week or more show a definite need for medical help:

1. Sleep problems, too much trouble falling asleep, early awakening.
2. Striking changes in eating habits; increased appetite and weight gain, or loss of appetite and weight loss.

3. Constant feeling of exhaustion.
4. Loss of pleasure in activities usually enjoyed.
5. Withdrawal from social activities.
6. Decreased sexual desire (teenagers may show marked increase).
7. Inability to concentrate.
8. Indecisiveness.
9. Feelings of helplessness.
10. Feelings of worthlessness.
11. Feelings of guilt.
12. Fearfulness, suspiciousness.
13. Restlessness, agitation.
14. Tearfulness.
15. Irritability.
16. Anxiety.
17. Persistent feeling of sadness.
18. Sad, droopy face.
19. Absorption in physical complaints.
20. Delusions of poverty.
21. Recurrent thoughts of death from disease.
22. Recurrent thoughts of suicide.

Psychoanalysis, a long and expensive form of treatment, is declining in popularity and in the number of physicians devoted exclusively to it. Some of the theories of its founder, Sigmund Freud, have recently been questioned, rightly or wrongly, on the basis of his intellectual honesty. Although it will likely continue to have a place in the treatment of some mental disorders, the trend is away from the older concepts toward new diagnostic techniques, with newer drugs aided by special short-term therapy.

Types of depression vary widely with full-scale "major depression" affecting about 1 in every 29 Americans. According to Dr. Keith H. Brodie, president of the American Psychiatric Association, "We don't know if the mind thinking depressed thoughts causes . . . biochemical changes or whether the chemical imbalance in the brain . . . causes the depression." Although there exists a wide range of depression therapies, there is a growing consensus that patients with major depression require specific drugs. Those most commonly prescribed are the tricyclic antidepressants, but others have recently been added to the list of oral prescription drugs known to affect chemical changes in the part of the brain where emotional responses originate. Most of these take about two weeks to begin lifting a depression, and for some patients, a class of drugs called monoamine oxidase inhibitors seems to be more effective.

In any case, the discovery that depression and most mental illnesses can be treated on a chemical basis has revolutionized the attitudes of patients and their families, bringing new hope of a return to normalcy for countless thousands whose lives had been on the road to self-destruction. But make no mistake:

Management of mental illness should always be under the direction of doctors of medicine with special training aided, of course, by skilled nurses, caring family members, and highly trained psychotherapists. As with other types of illness, risks must be evaluated and tragedies prevented if possible. Faddists or self-styled "experts" in this delicate field of illness must be absolutely avoided.

Even under the optimal care of physicians, there are patients who do not respond well to any method of treatment. But it is the trained physician who is in the best position to guide patients through the often serious phases of a mental illness toward the goal of recovery.

Alabama	University of Alabama Medical Center 619 South 19th Street University Station Birmingham, AL 35294 (205) 934-5171 Program Director: Dr. Patrick H. Linton
Arizona	University of Arizona Health Sciences Center 1501 North Campbell Avenue Tucson, AZ 85724 (602) 626-0111 Program Director: Dr. John Racy
California	University of California San Francisco Hospitals and Clinics 505 Parnassus Avenue San Francisco, CA 94143 (415) 476-1000 Program Director: Dr. Samuel Barondes
	Cedars-Sinai Medical Center 8700 Beverly Boulevard Los Angeles, CA 90048 (213) 855-5000 Program Director: Dr. Bert James Schloss
	Neuropsychiatric Institute University of California Los Angeles Medical Center 760 Westwood Plaza Los Angeles, CA 90024 (213) 825-0511 Program Director: Dr. Joel Yager
Colorado	University of Colorado Health Sciences Center 4200 East Ninth Avenue Denver, CO 80262 (303) 329-3066 Program Director: Dr. James H. Shore

Connecticut	Institute of Living 200 Retreat Avenue Hartford, CT 06106 (203) 241-8000 Program Director: Dr. Peter Zeman
	Yale Psychiatric Institute Huntington and Prospect Streets Box 12-A, Yale Station New Haven, CT 06520 (203) 436-1599 Program Director: Dr. Malcolm B. Bowers
District of Columbia	St. Elizabeth's Hospital 2700 Martin Lurther King, Jr., Drive Washington, DC 20032 (202) 574-7166 Program Director: Dr. Roger Peele
Florida	Shands Hospital—University of Florida 1600 S. W. Archer Road Gainesville, FL 32610 (904) 395-0111 Program Director: Dr. John Kuldau
	Jackson Memorial Hospital 1611 N. W. 12th Avenue Miami, FL 33136 (305) 325-7429 Program Director: Dr. Richard Steinbook
Georgia	Georgia Mental Health Institute Emory University Hospital 1364 Clifton Road, N. E. Atlanta, GA 30322 (404) 727-7021 Program Director: Dr. Donald E. Manning
Illinois	Illinois State Psychiatric Institute 1601 West Taylor Street Chicago, IL 60612 (312) 996-1000 Program Director: Dr. Lee Weiss
	Northwestern Institute of Psychiatry 250 East Superior Street Chicago, IL 60611 (312) 908-8058 Program Director: Dr. Leon Diamond

Southern Illinois University School of Medicine
801 North Rutledge/P. O. Box 19230
Springfield, IL 62794
(217) 782-3318
Program Director: Dr. Raymond Bland
(Special interests: multidisciplinary approach to diagnosis and treatment of Alzheimer's disease)

Iowa

University of Iowa Hospitals and Clinics
650 Newton Road
Iowa City, IA 52242
(319) 356-1533
Program Director: Dr. George Winokur

Kansas

C. F. Menninger Memorial Hospital
5800 West Sixth Street
Topeka, KS 66601
(913) 273-7500
Program Director: Dr. Efrain Bleiberg

Louisiana

Alton Ochsner Medical Foundation
1516 Jefferson Highway
New Orleans, LA 70121
(504) 838-3000
Program Director: Dr. Charles K. Billings

Maryland

Johns Hopkins Hospital
600 North Wolfe Street
Baltimore, MD 21205
(301) 955-5000
Program Director: Dr. Phillip Slavney

Massachusetts

McLean Hospital
115 Mill Street
Belmont, MA 02178
(617) 855-2000
Program Director: Dr. Phillip Isenberg

Erich Lindemann Mental Health Center
Massachusetts General Hospital
32 Fruit Street
Boston, MA 02114
(617) 726-2000
Program Director: Dr. Jonathan Borus

Massachusetts Mental Health Center
74 Fernwood Road
Boston, MA 02115
(617) 734-1300
Program Director: Dr. Jules Bemporad

Austen Riggs Center
Main Street
Stockbridge, MA 01262
(413) 298-5511
Program Director: James L. Sacksteder

Michigan   Detroit Psychiatric Institute
1151 Taylor Street
Detroit, MI 48202
(313) 874-4400
Program Director: Dr. Linn Campbell

Lafayette Clinic
951 East Lafayette Street
Detroit, MI 48207
(313) 256-9350
Program Director: Dr. C. E. Schorer

New Hampshire   Dartmouth-Hitchcock Medical Center
2 Maynard Street
Hanover, NH 03756
(603) 646-5000
Program Director: Dr. Peter Silverfarb

New Jersey   Trenton Psychiatric Hospital
P. O. Box 7500
West Trenton, NJ 08628
(609) 396-8261
Program Director: Dr. Rosalinda Gabriel

New Mexico   University of New Mexico Hospitals
2211 Lomas Boulevard, N. E.
Albuquerque, NM 87106
(505) 843-2111
Program Director: Dr. E. H. Ulenhuth

New York   New York State Psychiatric Institute
Columbia-Presbyterian Medical Center
622 West 168th Street
New York, NY 10032
(212) 305-2500
Program Director: Dr. Ronald Rieder

New York Hospital–Cornell Medical Center
525 East 68th Street
New York, NY 10021
(212) 746-5454
Program Director: Dr. Arnold Cooper

Manhattan Psychiatric Institute
600 East 125th Street
New York, NY 10035
(212) 369-0500
Program Director: Dr. Kenneth Kahaner

Hospital of the Albert Einstein College of Medicine
1500 Waters Place
New York, NY 10461
(718) 430-2000
Program Director: Dr. Joel S. Feiner

North Carolina   Duke University Medical Center
Box 3903
Durham, NC 27710
(919) 684-5587
Program Director: Dr. Alan A. Maltbie

University of North Carolina School of Medicine
Chapel Hill, NC 27514
(919) 966-4161
Program Director: Dr. Preston Walker

Ohio   Case Western Reserve University Hospital
Psychiatric Institute
2145 Adelbert Road
Cleveland, OH 44106
(216) 368-2450
Program Director: Dr. Robert C. Frymier

Pennsylvania   Hahnemann University Hospital
Department of Mental Health Services
Broad and Vine Streets
Philadelphia, PA 19102
(215) 448-7000
Program Director: Dr. Edward A. Volkman

Institute of Pennsylvania Hospital
111 North 49th Street
Philadelphia, PA 19139
(215) 471-2000
Program Director: Dr. Melvin Singer

Western Psychiatric Institute and Clinic
University of Pittsburgh Medical and Health Care Division
3811 O'Hara Street
Pittsburgh, PA 15213
(412) 624-3530
Program Director: Dr. Michael D. Rancurello

Tennessee   Maharry Community Mental Health Center
1005 David B. Todd Boulevard
Nashville, TN 37208
(615) 327-6218
Program Director: Dr. Harold Jordan

Texas   Texas Research Institute of Mental Sciences
1300 Moursund Boulevard
Houston, TX 77030
(713) 797-1976
Program Director: Dr. Mohsen Mirabi

Timberlawn Psychiatric Hospital
4600 Samuell Boulevard
Dallas, TX 75223
(214) 381-7181
Program Director: Dr. Keith Johansen

Virginia   Community Mental Health Center and Psychiatric Institute
721 Fairfax Avenue
Norfolk, VA 23501
(804) 446-5000
Program Director: Dr. Robert Vidaver

Wisconsin   Milwaukee Psychiatric Hospital
1220 Dewey Avenue
Milwaukee, WI 53213
(414) 258-2600
Program Director: Dr. Frank Johnson

· 13 ·

REHABILITATION: THE
COMEBACK TRAIL

Facing permanent disability, paralysis to any degree, or chronic pain can be the most difficult condition anyone must learn to accept, but Americans are blessed with what is probably the world's greatest variety of rehabilitation institutions. These centers are dedicated to restoring self-sufficiency and independence to the disabled and the handicapped of all ages—from the tiny victims of birth defects to children and adults who are hurt by accident, disease, war, or natural disaster.

Perhaps no effort organized for the benefit of mankind encompasses more devotion and man-hours than that represented by the U.S. Commission on Accreditation of Rehabilitation Facilities (CARF). Its sponsoring members include the American Hospital Association, Goodwill Industries of America, the National Association of Jewish Vocational Services, the National Easter Seal Society, and the United Cerebral Palsy Associations; associated members include the American Academy of Physical Medicine and Rehabilitation, the National Association of Rehabilitation Facilities, and the National Rehabilitation Association.

Within these national organizations, a community-based network of CARF-approved facilities and independent centers exists in every part of the country. Many are geared to specialized programs and have innovative services added yearly. As an example, the noted Harmarville Rehabilitation Center in Pittsburgh has recently introduced units for head injury, coma management, and mid-life stroke. Spinal cord injury centers are also available.

A study of these recovery centers, in fact, will reveal that no case of human disability is considered hopeless by the highly trained technicians who serve in them. Advances make new treatments possible in technological laboratories, where electricity is being used to diagnose and treat venous diseases, as well as to improve body movement, ambulation, and muscle-conditioning with computerized functional electrical stimulation.

Over 800 CARF centers in the United States are devoted to the training of children and adults with developmental difficulties, and all are located in easy-to-reach places. The presence of a center's name on the CARF list means that it complies with the highest standards of professionalism. Your doctor or your local hospital can help you to locate the best one near you. The coded letters used in the listing of some outsanding CARF-approved rehabilitation institutions have the following meanings:

AS	Activity services and goal-oriented therapy services designed to help individuals function in self-care and prevocational skills
Aud	Audiology emphasized with medical, social, and vocational skills
CP-0	
CP-1	Programs organized to deal with chronic pain
CP-1/0	
HBR	Hospital-based rehabilitation
IEC	Infant and early childhood developmental programs
ILP	Independent living programs
JP	Job placement
OMR	Outpatient medical restoration
OST	Occupational skill training
PR	Physical restoration
PSD	Personal and social development
PSP	Psycho-social programs and community adjustment for former psychiatric patients
RS	Residential services as part of self-help and independent programs
SCI	Spinal cord injury programs
SE	Sheltered employment
SP	Speech pathology
VE	Vocational evaluation
VocD	Vocational development supported by medical and social services
WA	Work activity supported by vocational, social, and personal services
WAdj	Work adjustment
WS	Work services (remunerative)

The following hospital-based rehabilitation facilities are recommended by CARF officials as "leaders, innovators, and trend-setters" in the vast field of human resources.

California   Rancho Los Amigos Hospital
7601 East Imperial Highway
Downey, CA 90242
(213) 922-7022
(HBR, VE)

Center of Rehabilitation Medicine
Northridge Hospital Medical Center
18300 Roscoe Boulevard
Northridge, CA 91328
(818) 885-8500
(HBR, SCI, CP-1/0, VE)

Casa Colina Hospital for Rehabilitation Medicine
255 East Bonita Avenue
Pomona, CA 91767
(714) 593-7521
(PR, SE)

Florida

Rehabilitation Institute of West Florida
1750 North Palafax Street
Pensacola, FL 32523
(904) 434-3481
(PR)

Georgia

Center for Rehabilitation Medicine
Emory University Hospital
1364 Clifton Road, N. E.
Atlanta, GA 30322
(404) 627-7021
(HBR, CP-1/0)

Roosevelt Warm Springs Institute for Rehabilitation
Warm Springs, GA 31830
(404) 655-3321
(HBR, VE, WAdj, OST, WS, ILP, PSP)

Illinois

Rehabilitation Institute of Chicago
345 East Superior Street
Chicago, IL 60611
(312) 908-6071
(HBR)

Rehabilitation Medicine Unit
Lutheran General Hospital
1775 Dempster Street
Park Ridge, IL 60068
(312) 696-2210
(HBR)

Center for the Rehabilitation and Training for the Disabled
2032 Clibourne Avenue
Chicago, IL 60646
(312) 929-8200

Massachusetts	Spaulding Rehabilitation Hospital 125 Nashua Street Boston, MA 02114 (617) 720-6400 (HBR, CP-1, PSP)
Michigan	Mary Free Bed Hospital and Rehabilitation Center 235 Wealthy, S. E. Grand Rapids, MI 49503 (616) 242-0300 (HBR)
	The Area Child Amputee Center 235 Wealthy Street Grand Rapids, MI 49503 (616) 454-7988
Minnesota	Sister Kenny Institute Abbot-Northwestern Hospital 800 East 28th Street Minneapolis, MN 55407 (612) 874-4000 (VocD, PR)
Missouri	Howard A. Rusk Rehabilitation Center University of Missouri Health Sciences Center One Hospital Drive Columbia, MO 65212 (314) 882-4141 (PR)
	Rehabilitation Institute and Physical Therapy for Arthritis 3011 Baltimore Avenue Kansas City, MO 64108 (816) 756-2250 (PR, VocD, SE)
New Jersey	Kessler Institute for Rehabilitation 1199 Pleasant Valley Way West Orange, NJ 07052 (210) 731-3600 (HBR)
New York	Institute of Rehabilitation Medicine 400 East 34th Street New York, NY 10016 (212) 340-7300 (HBR)

North Carolina	Charlotte Rehabilitation Hospital 1100 Blythe Boulevard Charlotte, NC 28203 (704) 333-6634 (HBR)
Ohio	Dodd Hall Ohio State University Hospitals 410 West Tenth Avenue Columbus, OH 43210 (614) 421-8000 (PR)
	Physical Medicine and Rehabilitation Center Good Samaritan Medical Center 800 Forest Avenue Zanesville, OH 43701 (614) 454-5000 (HBR, SCI, CP-0)
Oregon	Rehabilitation Institute of Oregon Good Samaritan Hospital and Medical Center 1015 N. W. 22nd Avenue Portland, OR 97210 (503) 229-7711 (HBR)
Pennsylvania	Moss Rehabilitation Hospital 12th Street and Tabor Road Philadelphia, PA 19141 (215) 329-5715 (PR)
	Harmarville Rehabilitation Center Box 11460 Guys Run Road Pittsburgh, PA 15238 (412) 781-5700 (PR, VocD)
	Rehabilitation Institute of Pittsburgh 6301 Northumberland Street Pittsburgh, PA 15217 (412) 521-9000 (HBR)

Texas   Institute for Rehabilitation and Research
                        1333 Moursund Boulevard
                        Houston, TX 77030
                        (713) 799-5000
                        (HBR)

Virginia   Woodrow Wilson Rehabilitation Center
                        Fishersville, VA 22939
                        (703) 885-9711
                        (PR, VocD, SP, Aud)

Wisconsin   Sacred Heart Rehabilitation Hospital
                        1545 South Layton Boulevard
                        Milwaukee, WI 53216
                        (414) 383-4490
                        (PR)

The following list is of rehabilitation facilities that are not based in hospitals.
They are vocationally oriented centers of excellence.

California   Hallelujah Corporation
                        La Mesa, CA 92041
                        (619) 464-2085
                        (VocD)

                        Mt. Diablo Rehabilitation Services
                        Pleasant Hill, CA 94523
                        (415) 682-6330
                        (OMR, VE, WAdj, OST, JP, WS)

                        Association for Retarded Citizens
                        5384 Linda Vista Road
                        San Diego, CA 92110
                        (619) 574-7575
                        (PSD, VocD, SE, WA)

Colorado   Goodwill Industries of Colorado Springs
                        2320 West Colorado Avenue
                        Colorado Springs, CO 80904
                        (719) 635-4483
                        (VocD, SE, WA)

Florida   Goodwill Industries Suncoast
                        10596 Gandy Boulevard, North
                        St. Petersburg, FL 33702
                        (813) 576-3819
                        (OST, VocD, SE, WA)

Idaho	Magic Valley Rehabilitation Services 484 Eastland Drive, South Twin Falls, ID 83301 (208) 734-4112 (VE, WAdj, JP, WS, AS)
Illinois	The Center for the Rehabilitation and Training of the Disabled 4001 West Devon Avenue Chicago, IL 60646 (312) 736-9303 (VE, WAdj, OST, JP, WE, AS, RS)
	Jewish Vocational Service and Employment Center One South Franklin Street Chicago, IL 60606 (312) 346-6700 (VE, WAdj, OST, JP, WS, AS)
Iowa	Hope Haven Area Development Center 1819 Douglas Avenue Burlington, IA 52601 (319) 753-6701 (SD, VocD, SE, WA)
Kansas	Developmental Services of Northwest Kansas East Highway 40 Hays, KS 67601 (913) 625-5678 (VocD, SE, PSD, WA)
	Kansas Elks Training Center 1006 East Walterman Street Wichita, KS 67211 (316) 269-7700 (VocD, SE, PSD, WA)
Michigan	Pine Rest Christina Rehabilitation Services 6850 South Division Grand Rapids, MI 49508 (616) 455-5900 (VE, VocD, JP, WS, AS, RS, PSP)
	E. B. I. Breakthru 821 Fourth Avenue Lake Odessa, MI 48849 (616) 374-8833 (VE, VocD, WAdj, JP, WS, AS, RS)

Minnesota	Mankato Rehabilitation Center 15 Map Drive Mankato, MN 56001 (507) 345-4507 (VocD, SE, WA)
New York	Federation Employment and Guidance Service 114 Fifth Avenue New York, NY 10011 (212) 741-7110 (VocD, SE, WA)
	International Center for the Disabled 349 East 24th Street New York, NY, 10011 (212) 679-0100 (PR, PSD, VocD, SP)
Ohio	Vocational Guidance and Rehabilitation Services 2239 East 55th Street Cleveland, OH 44103 (216) 431-7800 (VocD, SE)
Pennsylvania	Southeastern Pennsylvania Rehabilitation Center Elwyn Institute 111 Elwyn Road Elwyn, PA 19063 (215) 358-6400 (VocD, SE, WA, PSD, SP, Aud)
	Woods School Route 213 Langhorne, PA 19047 (215) 750-4000 (VE, WAdj, JP, WS, AS, RS)
	Vocational Rehabilitation Center of Allegheny County 1323 Forbes Avenue Pittsburgh, PA 15219 (412) 471-2600 (VE, WAdj, OST, JP, WS, PSP)
Tennessee	Bristol Regional Rehabilitation Center 714 State Street Bristol, TN 37620 (615) 968-3929 (VE, WAdj, JP, WS, AS, RS)

Wisconsin Goodwill Industries, Milwaukee Area
6055 North 91st Street
Milwaukee, WI 53225
(414) 353-6400
(VocD, SE, WA, PSD)

Rehabilitation Center of Sheboygan
1428 North Fifth Street
Sheboygan, WI 53081
(414) 459-3883
(VocD, SE, WA)

In scanning the preceding lists, the reader must also remember that the rehabilitation facilities named are leaders and innovators. The CARF-approved list, however, contains the names of hundreds of other excellent, community-based rehabilitation facilities in every state. In addition, many rheumatologists and orthopedic surgeons themselves have established therapy services to prepare their patients for the long road ahead. Our advice: Ask your doctor to recommend the best advanced-therapy centers in your own community.

SPINAL CORD INJURY CENTERS

The letters *SCI* on the CARF-approved lists indicate that these places have programs for paralyzed victims of spinal cord injury, who number an estimated 500,000 people in the United States. The importance of professional therapy services for this group of victims can hardly be overestimated.

Selected as a model by the Federal Rehabilitation Services Administration for its regional rehabilitation centers, the New England Regional Spinal Cord Injury Center at Boston University Hospital is noted for its disability training and its reputation for helping patients adjust to their paralysis.

For general information about spinal cord injury treatment centers in your area, write or call:

National Spinal Cord Injury Association
600 West Cummings Park Road
Suite 2000
Woburn, MA 01801
(617) 935-2722

Spinal Cord Society
2410 Lakeview Drive
Fergus Falls, MN 56537
(218) 739-5252

Some federally designated regional centers for the rehabilitation and treatment of spinal cord injury are:

Arizona	Good Samaritan Medical Center 1111 East McDowell Road Box 2989 Phoenix, AZ 85062 (602) 239-2000
California	Rancho Los Amigos Hospital 7601 East Imperial Highway Downey, CA 90242 (213) 922-7022
Colorado	Craig Hospital 3425 South Clarkson Street Englewood, CO 80110 (303) 789-8000
Florida	Spinal Cord Injury Rehabilitation Center University of Miami Affiliated Hospitals 1475 N. W. 12th Avenue Miami, FL 33136 (305) 547-6418
Georgia	Sheppard Spinal Clinic 2020 Peachtree Road Atlanta, GA 30309 (404) 352-2020
Illinois	Rehabilitation Institute of Chicago 345 East Superior Street Chicago, IL 60611 (312) 908-6071
Louisiana	Spinal Cord Injury Rehabilitation Center Louisiana State University Hospital 1541 Kings Highway Shreveport, LA 71130 (318) 674-5000
Massachusetts	New England Regional Spinal Cord Injury Center University Hospital 88 East Concord Street Boston, MA 02118 (617) 638-8000
Minnesota	Mayo Clinic 200 S. W. First Street Rochester, MN 55905 (507) 284-2511

New York	Spinal Cord Injury Rehabilitation Center Strong Memorial Hospital 601 Elmwood Avenue Rochester, NY 14642 (716) 275-2644
	Rusk Rehabilitation Center 400 East 34th Street New York, NY 10016 (212) 340-7300
North Dakota	Medical Center Rehabilitation Hospital 1300 South Columbia Road Grand Forks, ND 58201 (701) 780-5000
Pennsylvania	Thomas Jefferson University Hospital 11th and Walnut Streets Philadelphia, PA 19107 (215) 928-6000
Texas	Baylor College of Medicine One Baylor Plaza Houston, TX 77030 (713) 798-4951
Virginia	Woodrow Wilson Rehabilitation Center University of Virginia Hospital Jefferson Park Avenue Charlottesville, VA 22908 (804) 924-0211
Washington	Spinal Injury Rehabilitation Center University Hospital 1959 N. E. Pacific Street Seattle, WA 98195 (206) 548-3300

· 14 ·
ALCOHOL AND DRUG
ADDICTION TREATMENT

It is currently estimated that more than 6 million Americans of both sexes and all ages are addicted to drugs in one form or another, including caffeine in coffee and cola—two recently researched substances affecting even small children. The tragedy of alcoholism and other abuse is the terrible toll of lives destroyed each year by addiction, and it's usually not only the addict who suffers. Few "social drinkers" are aware of the effects of their drinking on their children or their grandchildren; nor are they aware that alcohol is just as much a drug as cocaine, heroin, marijuana, LSD, and prescription drugs.

Despite the worldwide spread of illegal drugs, it is heartening to note the rising number of addiction treatment centers of all types and in all parts of the country. Many of these treatment programs are free or are federally funded, for those unable to pay.

However grim the statistics in the very real "war on drugs," the "getting straight" movement, said to have its origins in former first lady Betty Ford's public announcement that she was entering a hospital for treatment of her addiction to pain-killers and alcohol, has grown steadily. Partly because of Mrs. Ford's candor and spirit, much of the shame and stigma attached to drug addiction has been removed. Changes in public and professional attitudes have brought a steady increase in the number of treatment centers, including the Betty Ford Treatment Facility at the Eisenhower Medical Center near Palm Springs, California, where scores of celebrities have been treated. Another former first lady, Nancy Reagan, provided educational drives in elementary schools during the 1980s with her "Just say no" slogan. In 1988 the International Summer Olympics Games Committee in Korea dramatized for millions the abuse of steroids by world-class athletes by expelling several star competitors. Drug and alcohol addicts, who used to be regarded from a moralistic standpoint, are now treated as victims of a disease. Consequently more and more people are openly seeking professional help, according to Dr. G. Douglas Talbot, director of the

Ridgeview Institute of Chemical Dependency for drug-impaired physicians located in Smyrna, Georgia.

In searching for treatment, the importance of choosing the right facility cannot be overemphasized, either can reliance on a trusted peer group to help. The basics of drug-dependency treatment remain pretty much the same wherever it takes place: detoxification (a must, with or without medication) to remove the poisons from the body of an addicted individual; group therapy, family counseling, and long-term (sometimes lifetime) participation in a self-help group such as Alcoholics or Narcotics Anonymous.

Membership in AA, which has thousands of local community chapters, has more than quadrupled since the late 1960s, and the organization has lately become increasingly involved with treatment of cocaine abusers. (Statistics show that in between 1976 and 1981 alone, there was a 600 percent rise in the number of cocaine addicts seeking help in publicly funded programs.)

As proof of the vast need for addiction treatment, a public information toll-free hot line (established in 1983 by Dr. Mark Gold, chief of research at Fair Oaks Hospital, a drug dependency hospital in Summit, New Jersey) receives well over 1,000 calls per day from addicts seeking help. The number to call is 800-COCAINE, and the telephones are answered 24 hours a day. The volunteers include many former addicts, and callers are given a computerized listing of over 700 doctors and drug-treatment centers across the country.

Other general facts about addiction treatment programs in the United States which addicts, their families, and their employers should know about include:

1. Probably the most complete and informative listing of qualified drug and alcohol treatment centers in the United States (some in Canada, Puerto Rico, and the Virgin Islands) is the National Alcohol and Drug Treatment Programs Directory, published by *U.S. Journal—Health Communications* in Florida. This book contains approximately 2,000 listings, with full information on the size of each center, its location, and the type of program. For further information, write or telephone Michael Miller, Vice President of Program Development, at (305) 429-9085. To order a copy, send $5 to:

   > National Alcohol and Drug Treatment Programs Directory
   > Enterprise Center
   > 3201 S. W. 15th Street
   > Deerfield Beach, FL 33442

   Focus and *Changes* magazines, for families affected by chemical dependency, are published by the same organization.
2. Some insurance companies provide coverage for alcohol abuse programs. Blue Cross and Blue Shield provides broad substance abuse benefits, which cover up to 165 days of treatment—ample time for many addicts to get themselves well on the way to recovery.

3. Employment assistance programs (EAPs) have been established by many large corporations. Substance abusers may include top executives and highly paid professionals, and cost of treatment programs can run as high as $350 a day.

4. Choosing the right rehabilitation facility for the individual alcoholic or other drug abuser is vitally important, because reliance on the particular group is one of the all-important parts of individual recovery. Whether it is an exclusive mountain-top hideaway or a community AA meeting in a local church, trust in the group is an essential factor in successful treatment.

California has always been at the forefront of treatment of alcohol and drug abuse, with an outstanding number of centers throughout the state. Many of these are nonprofit or operate at minimal cost. The moderate-cost Comprehensive Care Corporation opened its first Care Unit Hospital in Newport Beach in 1972 and has now expanded to more than 175 care units in 42 states. The Haight-Ashbury Free Medical Clinic in San Francisco, founded in 1967 by its present director, Dr. David Smith, is also a pioneer dating back to the 1960s. It has now expanded to include seven buildings, operating above capacity at all times. Its patients come from all walks of life—there are a number of therapy groups for doctors, lawyers, artists, and other professionals. Counterpoint Centers provide specialized help for adults, young adults, and adolescents with chemical abuse problems in more than seven states including California, Florida, Georgia, Idaho, Indiana, Louisiana, Mississippi, and Missouri. We can't stress strongly enough the fact that qualified professional treatment centers are available in every state in the Union, including hundreds located within hospitals.

Some private treatment centers are designed to appeal to special tastes and backgrounds, such as the Aspen Addiction Rehabilitation Unit of the Presbyterian–St. Lukes Medical Center in Aspen, Colorado, where strenuous outdoor activities like cross-country skiing, rock climbing, rope-crossing, and log-rolling teach reliance on others. Ten patients at a time are treated in a 28-day period, housed in a remodeled ranch at the base of Buttermilk Mountain.

The Colorado Rockies are also home to a number of other top-quality alcohol and drug treatment centers. In Boulder, the Boulder Memorial Hospital is noted for its "one day at a time" therapy regime in which patients practice yoga, meditation, and aquatic relaxation each day. The Ark, another Colorado mountain retreat, is a family-oriented rehabilitation center, as is the Hazelden Foundation near Minneapolis, famous for including families in the rehabilitation treatment. Hanley Hazelden at St. Mary's Hospital in West Palm Beach, Florida, is a new branch center of the famous Minnesota facility.

Many professionals in the field of drug rehabilitation doubt that psychiatrists and doctors, who are too often prone to administer drugs to drug addicts and sometimes find it difficult to reach the user on his or her own terms, make the best directors of these centers. Experienced and skilled lay people are often therapists for addictions for a variety of other reasons, especially for their ability to view addicts as people rather than patients.

If you are a concerned family member (and addiction is always a family matter if there is a family), talk over the problem with the director or administrator of a treatment center near you. These directors also serve as referral experts in finding the right center and program for your situation.

The following list of recommended centers (in addition to those mentioned in the chapter text) offers a number of reliable starting points for the search for effective alcohol and drug treatment:

Alabama
Brookwood Lodges
2010 Brookwood Medical Center Drive
Birmingham, AL 35259
(205) 647-1945
Program Director: Morris Hamilton

Arizona
Camelback Hospital
7575 East Earl Drive
Scottsdale, AZ 85251
(602) 941-7500
Program Director: Dr. Robert Triana

California
Betty Ford Center
Eisenhower Medical Center
39000 Bob Hope Drive
El Rancho Mirag, CA 92064
(800) 854-9211 or (619) 340-0033
Program Director: Dr. James West

Scripps Clinic Alcohol and Chemical Dependency
    Program
10666 North Torey Pines Road
La Jolla, CA 92037
(619) 457-8586
Program Director: Ken McDonald

Scripps Memorial Hospital Alcoholism/Drug Treat-
    ment Center
9888 Genesee Avenue
La Jolla, CA 92037
(800) 382-HELP
Program Director: Regi Karns

Colorado
Parkside Lodge of Colorado
8801 Lipan Street
Thornton, CO 80229
(303) 429-0292
Program Director: Ron Drier

Parkside Lodge of Florence
521 West Fifth Street
Florence, CO 81226
(303) 784-4809
Program Director: Paula Burton (This is an extended-
    care facility for women.)

Connecticut   Parkside Lodge of Connecticut
Route 7
Canaan, CT 06018
(800) 822-2228
Program Director: John Reese

Florida   Palm Beach Institute
1014 North Olive Street
West Palm Beach, FL 33401
(407) 833-7553
Program Director: Jerry Singleton

Center for Recovery
John F. Kennedy Memorial Hospital
P. O. Box 1489
Lake Worth
Atlantis, FL 33460
(407) 965-7300
Program Director: Ivan Goldberg

Brookwood Recovery Center
P. O. Box 2388
Kissimmee, FL 32742
(305) 841-7071
Program Director: Bob Hinds

Counterpoint Center
St. John's River Hospital
6300 Beach Boulevard
Jacksonville, FL 32216
(904) 724-9202
Program Directors: Caroline Noyes, Thomas Heany
(This center also provides facilities for the treatment
    of adolescents.)

Hanley Hazelden Center
St. Mary's Hospital
West Palm Beach, FL 33407
(407) 848-1666
Program Director: Patrick Griffin

Georgia   Ridgeview Institute Chemical Dependency Program
3995 South Cobb Drive
Smyrna, GA 30080
(404) 434-4567
Program Director: Dr. G. Douglas Talbot

Counterpoint Center
1999 Cliff Valley Way
Atlanta, GA 30329
(404) 633-8431
Program Director: John Wilson

Illinois   Lutheran Center for Substance Abuse
1700 Luther Lane
Park Ridge, IL 60068
(312) 696-6050
Program Director: Rev. Carl Malin

Ingalls Center
Ingalls Memorial Hospital
One Ingalls Drive
Harvey, IL 60426
(312) 333-2300
Program Director: Dr. Harry Hanning

St. Mary's Hospital
Family Care Unit
1415 Vermont Street
Quincy, IL 62301
(217) 223-1200
Program Director: Tom Stalf

Indiana   Koala Center
1711 Lafayette Avenue
Lebanon, IN 46052
(317) 482-3711
Program Director: Robert Edwards

Koala Center
P. O. Box 1549
Columbus, IN 47202
(812) 376-1711
Program Director: John Solomon

Louisiana   Baton Rouge Chemical Dependency Program
4040 North Boulevard
Baton Rouge, LA 70806
(504) 387-7900
Program Director: Jim Milliken

Bowling Green Inn
701 Florida Avenue
Mandeville, LA 70448
(504) 626-5661
Program Director: George Rozelle

Maryland   Meadows Recovery Center
P. O. Box 521
730 Maryland Route 3
Gambrills, MD 21054
(301) 923-6022
Program Director: Jan Williams

Michigan   Brighton Hospital
12851 East Grand River Road
Brighton, MI 48116
(313) 227-1211
Program Director: Ivan Harner

Insight
420 West Fifth Avenue
Flint, MI 48503
(313) 733-5981
Program Director: Stephen Lebei

Minnesota   Parkview Youth/Family Center
14400 Martin Drive
Eden Prairie, MN 55344
(612) 934-7555
Program Director: John Hagen

Hazelden Foundation
Box 11
15245 Pleasant Valley Road
Center City, MN 55012
(612) 257-4010
Program Director: Dr. Daniel Anderson

Missouri   Baptist Medical Center
6601 Rockhill Road
Kansas City, MO 64131
(816) 361-8020
Program Directors: John Gallagher, Robert Darr

New Hampshire   Spofford Hall
                         P. O. Box 225
                         Route 9-A
                         Spofford, NH 03462
                         (603) 363-4545
                         Program Director: Wilma Reed Grimm

New Jersey   Fair Oaks Hospital
                         19 Prospect Street
                         Summit, NJ 07901
                         (201) 522-7000
                         Program Director: Richard Jensen

                         New Beginning
                         440 Beckerville Road
                         Lakehurst, NJ 08733
                         (201) 657-4800
                         Program Director: Elaine Luthringer

                         Seabrook House
                         P. O. Box 5055
                         Seabrook, NJ 08302
                         (609) 455-7575
                         Program Director: Charles Reinert

New York   Freeport Hospital Treatment Center
                         267 South Ocean Avenue
                         Freeport, NY 11520
                         (516) 328-0800
                         Program Director: Dr. Alan Herzlin

                         Parkview Treatment Center of New York
                         P. O. Box 37
                         Route 118
                         Yorktown Heights, NY 10598
                         (914) 962-5000
                         Program Director: Dr. Gordon Bohl

                         Smithers Alcoholism Treatment Center
                         428 West 59th Street
                         New York, NY 10019
                         (212) 554-6715
                         Program Director: Pamela Cavanaugh

Daytop Village
401 State Street
Brooklyn, NY 11201
(718) 625-1388
Program Director: Leigh Guilfoyle
(This center is especially known for the treatment of
    children.)

Pennsylvania   Richard Caron Foundation
Box 277
Galen Hall Road
Wernersville, PA 19565
(215) 678-2332
Program Director: Charles Beem

Valley Forge Medical Center and Hospital
1033 West Germantown Pike
Norristown, PA 19403
(215) 539-8500
Program Director: Joseph Pollack

ARC/The Terraces
Chemical Dependency Program
P. O. Box 729
Ephrata, PA 17522
(717) 627-0790
Program Director: Gerald Schulman

Ohio   Care Unit Hospital of Cincinnati
3156 Glenmore Avenue
Cincinnati, OH 45211
(513) 481-8822
Program Director: Larry Burge

Texas   Care Unit Hospital of Dallas/Ft. Worth
1066 West Magnolia Avenue
Ft. Worth, TX 76104
(817) 336-2828
Program Director: Marilyn Anderson

Chemical Dependency Unit of South Texas
5517 South Alameda
Corpus Christi, TX 78412
(512) 993-6100
Program Director: William Wigmore

Utah

Cottage Program
736 South 500 East
Salt Lake City, UT 84102
(800) 752-6102
Program Director: Bernell Boswell

Washington

Puget Sound Hospital
215 South 36th Street
Tacoma, WA 98408
(206) 474-0561
Program Director: Hugh Long

Wisconsin

Madison General Hospital
202 South Park Street
Madison, WI 53715
(608) 267-6000
Program Director: Brian Vogel

· 15 ·
EMERGENCY TRAVEL: HOW TO GET TO THE HOSPITAL OF YOUR CHOICE

Knowing *where* to go for the best medical treatment is what this book is all about. But in emergency situations or in cases of critical illness involving the transportation of a person from home to the hospital or from one hospital to another, knowing *how* to get there is of equal importance.

With time, distance, degree of illness, and costs all factors to consider in such emergency travel, air transportation (including helicopters) is, of course, the fastest way to go almost anywhere, and few among us would be bothered by the cost of an air ambulance when it may mean saving our lives or the life of someone we love.

Although such lifesaving services once were somewhat rare (and expensive to the average citizen), new emergency transport systems are now available in most parts of the United States. These systems are designed to save dollars as well as precious medical time. Thanks to American ingenuity and often to pure philanthropy by individuals, desperately ill people of all ages are now being flown from around the world to hospitals in the United States for delicate, lifesaving surgery that is often either partially covered by health insurance plans or free.

The most complete and possibly the fastest service ever offered to doctors and their patients is the pioneering University of Albama Hospitals' Critical Care Transport Service established in 1983. The brain child of Ralph Quentin Mitchell, Jr., director of the service in the Birmingham headquarters, this service transports by plane and by hospital-equipped van (within Alabama) any patient in the United States from home to hospital or from one hospital intensive-care unit to another where specialized treatment is ready and available. The Cessna Citation jets and hospital vans used are engineered and equipped to provide for the uninterrupted and complete intensive-care needs of each individual patient. Helicopter support is also provided when necessary through Alabama's Carraway Methodist Hospital's Life Saver program.

The most significant feature of this transport system, however, is the trained team of medical specialists assigned to stabilize the patient before departure, to maintain treatment en route, and to brief the receiving physician at the final destination. Typically the team includes a physician, an intensive-care unit nurse, and a respirator therapist. A pediatric team from the University of Alabama Medical Center's Children's Hospital is also available when necessary.

What do you do to arrange for a patient transfer? Simply call the toll-free University of Alabama Hospital's Transport hot line 1-800-452-9860 (in Alabama call 1-800-292-6508) and ask for the transport coordinator. With the aid of the transport control physician, the transport coordinator will make the arrangements for the safest, most efficient method of transportation and answer any questions you and your attending doctor may have.

The cost for the plane is a $180 basic charge plus $2.25 per round-trip mile. For the van there is a $75 basic charge plus $1.75 per round-trip mile. For both the nurse and the therapist the cost is $50 per hour. (In estimating cost, remember that the round-trip mileage is back to the Alabama home base). They will take patients anywhere, not just in Alabama.

Airlift Northwest, affiliated with the University of Washington's four hospitals and medical center in Seattle, provides complete air transportation for medical emergencies in Washington, Alaska, Montana, and Idaho. Both the jets and helicopters used are medically equipped and have two nurses aboard and a doctor when needed. Some 40 other major hospital centers provide fixed-wing air transportation, and 180 medical centers are affiliated with emergency helicopter ambulances.

Every state in the United States now has emergency air transport systems, all of which can be reached by the referring doctor through toll-free telephone numbers. Some states, in fact, have several such systems and most of these are listed under "Civil U.S. Air Medical Programs" published by *Hospital Aviation Magazine:*

> *Hospital Aviation Magazine*
> c/o Nord Perfect Publishing Corporation
> 228 West Center Street
> Orem, UT 84047
> (801) 226-5555

Send $3 for a copy of the magazine.

Your doctor can refer you or the patient to any hospital listed in these pages, at the same time arranging air transportation if needed. In any case, a knowledge of the available air medical service in your own state is important.

Possibly the *only* free (for patients who are unable to pay) nonprofit medical air transport service in the country is Mission Air, located in Charlotte, North Carolina. This service is a volunteer group of pilots, medical personnel, and social workers who will fly qualifying medical cases from one part of the United States to another on the recommendation of doctors, family members, or an investigative social worker. If you have a family member or a friend in desperate need of medical air transport within the United States who is unable to pay the high cost of air transport, you can call Mission Air at the Charlotte headquarters, (704) 332-9126, or have your doctor or social worker telephone for you; the investigative process will then be put into operation. This organization has a long record of successful transportation and is supported entirely by donation.

In general, the good news in moving a sick patient to a better facility is that most major medical insurance policies cover necessary transport costs to the nearest teaching or accredited hospital center (or in the case of severe burns to the nearest burn center). At the moment of crisis, however, it is up to the patient's family and physician to make the best choice of hospitals. For this reason, the more you know of the country's medical map as well as your regional hospital locations, the better your choice will be at the crucial time.

Air ambulances, equipped to transport medical patients, are often listed in the Yellow Pages, although their prices are not listed. These companies are authorized and regulated by the Federal Aviation Board, and the air ambulances carry needed medical equipment and personnel and make all ground-air arrangements. Your doctor or local hospital may recommend a reliable company, or you may want to consider one of the jet charter services if the family budget can stand the strain.

If not, there may be other alternatives such as CAN—Corporate Angels Network. CAN offers *free* transportation to ambulatory patients via corporate-owned jets on their regular runs to most cities in the United States. Nationally coordinated with a network of privately owned jets, the service will make all arrangements after your call to the White Plains headquarters: (914) 328-1313.

If you are lucky enough to work for one of the operations affiliated with this network, you may be able to make your own arrangements directly with those in charge. In the face of desperate need and serious illness, big companies do have hearts—as do some private, philanthropic individuals with their own private planes stabled in local flying fields. The manager of the field will know who they are and possibly how to approach them. If the distance to be traveled is not too great and there is time, it is possible to rent or borrow a motor home or camper that can be medically equipped to make the trip.

The main idea is to get the patient to the *best* in-state or out-of-state medical care he or she may require as soon as possible. Don't settle for second-best while there is time. Today's medical expertise is available to everyone, but it is usually up to you to seek it and to know something beforehand about where to go for the best care and how to get there!

INDEX